IMAGES
of Sport

ST HELENS
RUGBY LEAGUE CLUB

Second rower Chris Joynt, in Saints' centenary kit of blue and white striped jerseys, takes the ball up in their 24-14 Challenge Cup semi-final victory against Widnes at Central Park, Wigan, in 1996. St Helens staged the best recovery ever seen at Wembley several weeks later when they came back from being 26-12 down going into the last twenty-three minutes, beating Bradford Bulls by 40-32. A superb hard-running and tackling second rower, Chris went up to lift the trophy himself twelve months later after a sporting gesture by Bobbie Goulding, who had been suspended during the earlier rounds. Joynt's tremendous 21-tackle performance was capped by a magnificent try in the forty-ninth minute, which gave Saints a vital 12-point advantage. A Great Britain Test player of distinction, Chris was the captain and heartbeat of the St Helens side as the game approached the new millennium.

2

IMAGES
of Sport

ST HELENS
RUGBY LEAGUE CLUB

Compiled by
Alex Service

TEMPUS

First published 2000
Copyright ©Alex Service, 2000

Tempus Publishing Limited
The Mill, Brimscombe Port,
Stroud, Gloucestershire, GL5 2QG

ISBN 0 7524 1883 1

Typesetting and origination by
Tempus Publishing Limited
Printed in Great Britain by
Midway Clark Printing, Wiltshire

This book is dedicated to the Red and White Army who follow the Saints wherever they play ... come hell or high waters. Despite changes in the whole fabric of the 'Greatest Game' over the past decade, these people are its very life-blood. Never believe otherwise.

Also available from Tempus Publishing

Bradford RLFC	Robert Gate	Summer 2000
Castleford RLFC	David Smart	Summer 2000
Halifax RLFC	Andrew Hardcastle	0 7524 1831 9
Headingley Voices	Phil Caplan	0 7524 1822 X
Hunslet RLFC	Les Hoole	0 7524 1641 3
Leeds RLFC	Phil Caplan & Les Hoole	0 7524 1140 3
Sheffield Eagles RLFC	John Cornwell	0 7524 1830 0
Warrington RLFC	Eddie Fuller & Gary Slater	0 7524 1870 X
Salford RLFC	Graham Morris	Summer 2000
The Five Nations Story	David Hands	0 7524 1851 3
Anfield Voices	David Paul	0 7524 1114 4
Burnley FC	Ray Simpson	0 7524 1520 4
Bury FC	Peter Cullen	0 7524 1526 3
Crewe Alexandra FC	Harold Finch	0 7524 1545 X
Final Tie	Norman Shiel	0 7524 1669 3
Goodison Park Voices	David Paul	0 7524 1548 4
Hull City FC	Chris Elton	0 7524 1620 0
Leeds United FC	David Saffer	0 7524 1642 1
Sheffield United FC	Denis Clareborough	0 7524 1059 8
Tranmere Rovers	Peter Bishop	0 7524 1505 9

(All books are 128 page softbacks with the exception of *The Five Nations Story* which is a 176 page hardback with colour illustrations.)

Contents

Kel Coslett.

Foreword

It is indeed a great honour for a boy from the Valleys to be asked to introduce this pictorial history of the Saints – a club for which I left my home in Bynea, thirty odd years ago, never thinking that it would become such an important part of my life even to this day. Alex's slices of the past will interest all generations of Saints' fans, but it allowed me to reflect on two decades of unbroken success, the 1960s and 1970s, when the Saints reigned supreme. His photographs bring to mind that great team of 1966, which boasted players of the calibre of Vollenhoven and Killeen, Warlow and Watson, Murphy and Bishop, and which resulted in winning the four cups. Ten years on and with the Challenge Cup once again in my hands, I was part of another great side. More local lads this time, with the likes of Benyon, Chisnall, Jones, Pimblett and Heaton, adding to the Welsh influence of Mantle and Mathias. Wonderful memories, wonderful players and friends.

I am sure that Rugby League spectators everywhere will enjoy these glimpses of one of its finest clubs, whilst Saints' fans will find their memories flooding back to the teams and glories of their 'own' Saints.

Kel Coslett
November 1999

Introduction

St Helens is the greatest Rugby League club in the world. You want proof? Just ask any dyed-in-the-wool Saints fanatics like me and you will be told in no uncertain terms what this sporting organisation means to us. It is what gives our proud town a place on the sporting map of the world, from Warrington to Woolongong.

Compiling a pictorial history about such a famous club is really a dream come true. Yet given the club's tremendous success and rightful place in the British Rugby League elite for the last fifty years, it is inevitable that such a publication can only provide a snapshot of different eras, great matches and great players.

Choice of themes is, in itself, a difficult task. The Saints were founder members of the breakaway Northern Union in 1895 and took part in the first-ever Challenge Cup final, two years later. The period between the wars was a veritable golden age, with two teams vying for glory in the town – the Saints and the Recs, the Pilkington works team. By a bitter irony, the Recs won a major honour before the Saints did. The town team rode the general depression of the late 1930s, although this was at the expense of the disbanded Recs. The club joined the elite with the introduction of Jim Sullivan as coach in 1952. A period of continual success beckoned for the next thirty years.

The Saints have played their part in some memorable Challenge Cup finals and these great moments from Wembley are dealt with, from the club's first visit in 1930 to the turning over of the Bradford Bulls in 1997 – St Helens' first back-to-back success.

The 1960s and 1970s were memorable decades for Saints' fans, with success and a seemingly endless supply of star players reflected by numerous call-ups for county and country. There have been many great overseas players donning the famous red and white jersey over the years too – such as Van Vollenhoven, Meninga and Tuilagi – adding that extra-special ingredient which pulls in the crowds.

In the 1980s and early 1990s the club enjoyed a reputation for fast, open football. Yet entertainers do not necessarily enjoy the fruits of success. Arguably, a more pragmatic, less cavalier approach would have produced more silverware. Despite the disappointments, it remains one of the most interesting eras in the club's history.

St Helens' whole existence was turned upside-down in 1996, with the change to summer rugby, something that the Saints had been talking about in the late 1960s. Despite disorientated body-clocks, the team and club embraced the concept of a Super League with a magnificent League and Challenge Cup double – the first for twenty years. Fans travelled to Wales, London and Paris, some in lieu of summer holidays, to follow the team. In fact, the sight of so many thousands of Saints' fans at the Charlety Stadium in Paris, during the run-in to the 1996 title, is a memory which will stay with me forever.

And then there is the 'Field of Dreams' itself, Knowsley Road. We are fiercely proud of our ground, one of the best places to watch the 'Greatest Game' – choc full of character, well-appointed and with an intimacy all of its own, friendly yet foreboding for the opposition. This is the place where we pay homage to our sporting heroes. It is part of our heritage and somewhere which is almost as familiar to us as our own home. There are thousands just like me in the town who have been introduced to their 'second home' at a tender age and it has remained an integral part of their lives ever since. We even watch the match from our own special vantage point – the Edington Kop in my case – and rarely, if ever, deviate from our appointed 'spec'.

The new millennium will see a new stadium for the Saints, although not necessarily at Knowsley Road. It has got to be right for everyone concerned. You cannot ignore progress, but once the bulldozers come in, there will be no turning back. However, I remain optimistic for the future of this great club. As a Sintelliner, born and bred, it will always be the only one for me.

This club means so many different things to so many people. I hope you enjoy this pictorial excursion down memory lane, and that it triggers-off your own particular recollections of the greatest team in the greatest game.

Alex Service
September 1999

Acknowledgements

There are many people who have contributed, both directly and indirectly, to the completion of this book and if I have left anyone out it is certainly not intentional. The photographic files of the *St Helens Reporter* and the *St Helens Star* have provided valuable images, without which this book would never have got off the ground. The *Rugby Leaguer* too, now enjoying its half-century, has been a most valuable picture source. Rugby League historian Robert Gate has allowed me to use some of his remarkable archive material, together with Saints collector Curtis Johnstone. I would also like to place on record my thanks to Bernard Platt, Brian Peers, Gerald Webster, Denis Whittle, Ron Hoofe, Steve Llewellyn, Leslie Fairclough and, of course, Kel Coslett for the foreword. Geoff Pimblett and the Saints Past Players' Association have also been extremely supportive. Grateful thanks also go to Max Woosey and his staff at Knowsley Road for putting up with me in the role of 'enthusiastic amateur photographer'. The pictorial ground archive is considerably richer as a result.

Alex Service
March 2000

One
Early Days
1873-1918

PASSING THE BALL

This is how typical Northern Union footballers would look in 1895. Notice the long shorts kept up by a 'snake belt' and the boots drawn without bars across the soles – quite probably artistic licence. The game itself was Rugby Union initially, the only difference being the award of 'broken time' payments for men who had to miss work to play on Saturday afternoons.

FOOTBALL.

St. Helens v. Liverpool Royal Infirmary.—The announcement of this match, the first that has ever been played in St. Helens, excepting amongst members of the town club, attracted to the ground a large number of spectators, who evinced a hearty appreciation of the peculiarly characteristic features of the game, their enthusiasm being but very slightly damped by a smart shower of hail. The ball was kicked off at 3-30 by the home team; the strangers, who were several men short, winning the toss, selected the upper goal, and so secured the advantage of playing with the wind. Thus aided, the capital play of their forwards enabled them to keep the ball in rather close proximity to their opponents' goal, and but for the strength of the back players must infallibly have gained some more decided advantage than the four touch-downs they scored by half-time. On ends being changed the aspect of affairs was for a time entirely altered, the ball being carried down into the heart of the "Royals'" territory. This however did not last long, the superior training and backing up of the Liverpool team gaining ground for them in all the scrummages, the excellence of their forward play going far to neutralize the disparity of numbers, as they were able to dispense with all their back players but one, whilst St. Helens had no less than seven. On "no side" being called the Liverpool men had added another touch-down to their score, a very pleasant game thus terminating in a draw in their favour. Where all played so well it is difficult to particularise individual merit, but we would wish to call attention to the rule much neglected by both clubs that, "In the event of any player holding or running with the ball being tackled, and the ball fairly held, he must at once cry *down* and then put it down," instead of wasting time in mauling, which on Saturday was far too prevalent.

The players for St. Helens were:—

W. D. Herman (captain, three-quarters back)	D. Gamble
J. T. Roberts ⎫	W. Gamble
R. Thomas ⎬ (backs)	M. Hammill
T. Bell ⎭	E. Jackson
J. Hammill ⎫	D. E. Jones
J. Bishop ⎬ (half-backs)	J. Pritchard
H. Varley ⎭	W. R. Thomson
J. Broome	R. Varley
G. Bushby	W. Varley
J. Forster	C. C. Wilson

The very first rugby match played by a St Helens team, against Liverpool Royal Infirmary, as reported in the *St Helens Standard*, 31 January 1874. The club was founded by William Douglas Herman, a chemist at Pilkington's Crown Glassworks in the town, during a public meeting at the Fleece Hotel on Wednesday 19 November 1873. Under the chairmanship of Douglas Herman, the side played its first matches on the Recreation Cricket Ground at Boundary Road. What a different game it was then: twenty-a-side, with thirteen forwards and the only method of scoring was by kicks at goal. The try existed, but simply as a means of winning the right to 'try' a kick at goal. It was possible for a team to score a number of tries and convert none, while their opponents might score a single try, convert it, and win the match. Although Liverpool Infirmary registered five touchdowns to nil, these were not converted and the game ended in a 'draw in their favour'.

A fine body of men! The St Helens Rangers, in their black jerseys and long breeches, strike a splendid pose outside the old Abbey Hotel, *c.* 1882/83. Captain Alec Borthwick sits proudly on the right. Notice the player with 'S.H.R.' on his jersey – positive identification of this early version of the Saints! It was about this time that the Rangers had come to an agreement with the St Helens Cricket Club for a playing pitch on their field off Bishop Road, Dentons Green. Matches with local rivals St Helens Recreation, the club founded by Pilkington Brothers Glassworks, were being played there by the early 1880s. In 1885, the St Helens Rangers became the St Helens Rugby Football Club and could boast an impressive list of patrons and vice-presidents. These included the Earl of Derby (the borough MP), as well as great industrialists Sir Joseph Beecham and members of the Pilkington and Gamble families. On a Thursday evening in January 1889, St Helens played Wigan in the town's first-ever floodlit match in front of over 7,000 spectators at Dentons Green. The ground was illuminated by twelve Wells patent electric lamps, whilst the entrance to the field was lit up by another two. The fine weather ensured the venture was a complete success. Wigan, assisted by county centre Jack Hurst of Leigh, won an exciting match by 2 goals, 1 try, and 3 minors to 1 goal and 2 minors. Minor points were awarded when a defender was forced into his own touch-in-goal. On 14 March 1889, the club played host to their first overseas visitors, the New Zealand Maoris, in front of 5,000 at Dentons Green. The visitors won quite comfortably, with an impressive display of forward power. The forwards were the attackers in those days and had no fixed positions. In the scrummages it was a case of first on the scene, first down. The object of each scrum member was to use his weight or skill in dribbling, to drive the ball forward and not to win it for his backs.

11

Proud to be Saints. Captain Billy Cross (holding the ball) and his team-mates, wearing their blue and white striped jerseys in front of the dressing hut at Knowsley Road, *c*. 1894/95. These colours were resurrected for the Rugby League centenary season in 1995. From left to right, back row: Mr T.C. Wilcock (chairman), J. Appleton, E. Ashcroft, W. Whiteley, J. Brownbill, W. Wilson, J. Gladwin, T. Sudlow, J. Edwards (official). Middle row: T. Foulkes, R. Doherty, F. Little, Rennie. Front row: P. Dale, W. Cross, Jones, Graham, J. Garrity (mascot).

Winger Bob Doherty's splendid blue velvet club cap, as worn in the team photograph above. Awarded in 1889, it remains in pristine condition today. Notice the town crest and inscription *Ex Terra Lucem*. Club caps were generally subscribed for by admirers of the players. In some cases, it was paid for by the player's workmates. 'Bob Doc' signed for St Helens from Kendal Hornets in the late 1880s and the crowd took him to their hearts. His tackling was exceptional for a small man and he could bring down opponents forty or fifty pounds heavier than himself.

The Saints' 'Flying Curate', Revd Christopher Chavasse, during his days at Oxford University. A former winger with Liverpool Rugby Union Club, Christopher was ordained in 1910 and appointed to the St Helens parish church staff. He played in the 'A' team as an amateur and was called-up into the first team for a match with Wakefield Trinity. When he did not appear, his place on the wing was taken by 'Butcher' Prescott, the reserve forward. About half an hour had passed when a figure in a blue and black jersey vaulted over the fence and rushed onto the field. It was the Flying Curate, but his stay was short-lived as the referee sent him off because St Helens already had thirteen men on the field. Much to his disgust, he was also reported for ungentlemanly conduct, not having first sought the referee's permission to enter the field of play. Christopher had fallen asleep while writing his sermon and had missed the wagonette to the ground. The affair was soon forgotten, however, and the future Bishop of Rochester went on to play three matches for St Helens, scoring three tries.

In the pre-Northern Union days of 1895, the St Helens club won its first major honour – the Lancashire County Rugby Challenge Cup Division Two, presented by the West Lancashire and Border Towns Rugby Union. It was handed over to Saints' Cumbrian skipper, Billy Cross, after the final match of the season against Tyldesley at Knowsley Road by St Helens' first-ever Member of Parliament, Henry Seton-Carr. The gleaming trophy cost in excess of seventy-five guineas and the players were later presented with personally inscribed commemorative gold medals. The medal in the picture belonged to Thatto Heath-born forward Ned Ashcroft and has remained in pristine condition ever since. That night, in response to the kind invitation of Mr Wallace Revill, the manager of the Theatre Royal, the team attended a performance of the drama, *It's Never Too Late To Mend*. I wonder whether such after-match entertainment would appeal to the modern-day Saints?

Making Rugby League history. Batley and St Helens contested the inaugural Challenge Cup final at Headingley, Leeds, on Saturday 24 April 1897. Both teams and officials lined-up together for the camera, in front of a packed main stand, with the gleaming new trophy as the centre-piece. Batley really look the part, clad in immaculate white shirts and black shorts, in three rows of five (it was still fifteen-a-side in those days), while the Saints adopt a more laid-back pose. St Helens, captained by full-back Tommy Foulkes (with ball), were a superstitious lot and wore what the *Athletic News* described as 'faded and washed-out blue and white hooped jerseys'. Mind you, it was unlikely that the hard-up St Helens committee would have purchased

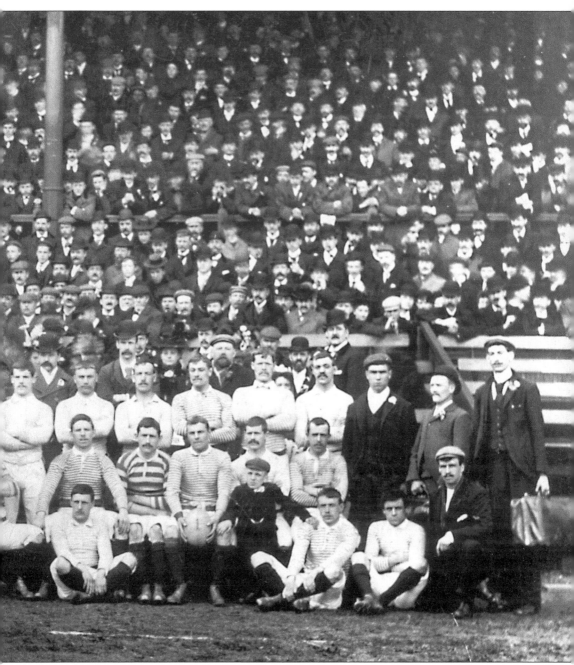

a new set anyhow. A century before Super League and the loveable St Bernard, the Saints had a dwarf mascot called Jimmy Garrity (seated next to Tom Foulkes in the front row). Not that he brought them much luck. Philistine, in the *Athletic News*, concluded that the Batley forward power had been the major factor on the day: 'The Batley forwards were too strong and too bull-necked for the men from St Helens, and the style in which the ultimate victors began their work told a tale in the first twenty minutes. Seven points to the good in that period against the wind was worth nearly seventy in the matter of enthusiasm, and Batley played like winners from the start.' The final score was Batley 10 St Helens 3.

ST. HELENS RUGBY FOOTBALL CLUB.

BALANCE SHEET, 1895-96.

Income.

	£ s. d.	£ s. d.
To Subscriptions...	86 16 0	
,, Gate Money ...	498 10 4	
,, Ground Account ...	17 11 0	
,, L. & N. W. Ry. Co.—Commission	14 18 11	
,, ,, 1894-95	10 10 0	
,, Insurance Account	49 0 0	
,, Half Fares Hull "A" Team, refunded	4 14 0	682 0 3
,, Balance due London and Midland Banking Co.	98 1 8	
,, Cash Advanced by Treasurer	46 18 4	145 0 0
		£827 0 3

Expenditure.

	£ s. d.
By Balance brought forward London and Midland Banking Co.	96 5 1
,, ,, due Secretary and Treasurer—1894-95	29 10
,, Teams' Travelling Expenses	136 19 1
,, Ground Account...	26 13
,, Rent, Rates, &c...	35 0
,, Players' Lost Time	106 2
,, Refreshments—Visiting Teams and Players	53 2
,, Money Takers and Checkers	17 18
,, Police	7 16
,, Referees and Touch Judges	39 14
,, Conveyances	5 15
,, Printing, Posting, &c.	43 15
,, Dress Account	38 12 1
,, Secretaries' Salary on Account...	10 0
,, Postages, Telegrams, &c.	10 4
,, Secretaries' and Delegates' Expenses	21 7
,, Insurance Paid for Injuries	55 16
,, Knee Caps, Bandages, &c...	1 16
,, Insurance Premium	45 7
,, Extra Cost of Medals	1 0
,, Northern Union—Subscriptions and Fines	10 14
,, Purchase of Refreshment Tents	8 10
,, Sundries	0 10
,, Paid Stand Account	20 0
,, Auditors' Fees—1894-95	1 1
,, Bank Interest and Commission, and Cheque Books	3 6
	£827 0

Liabilities.

	£ s. d.
London and Midland Banking Co....	98 1 8
P. Mearns, Esq.	62 0 0
Accounts Owing (Tradesmen)	126 3 1
Treasurer	46 18 4
Secretary	9 10 3
Treasurer's Salary	10 0 0
	£352 13 4

Assets.

	£ s. d.	£ s. d.
To Fencing, Stand, Pavilion, Turnstiles, &c.		190 0
,, Amount due from Sacred Heart	5 0 0	
,, ,, ,, Cricket Club, July 1st	2 10 0	7 10
,, Balance Deficiency		155 3
		£352 13

Audited and found Correct, 23rd June, 1896,

H. W. ROUGHLEY, } AUDITORS.
W. G. FOREMAN, }

Saints' balance sheet for 1895/96 included 'players' lost time' at the princely sum of just over £106. In the industrial north, clubs paid expenses to working men who forfeited a Saturday shift to play rugby. There were many who claimed they could not afford to play unless they were compensated for such lost time. These 'broken time' payments were no more than a few bob, yet over a century ago that counted for much when a sovereign had to keep many a family for a week. At the Rugby Union AGM in September 1893, a proposal that 'players be allowed compensation for bona fide loss of time', was defeated by 282 votes to 136. Despite this, the northern clubs insisted on paying broken time, which led to the famous split of 29 August 1895, when twenty-two clubs broke away from the parent body to form the Northern Rugby Football Union. Saints' first match in the new competition was at home to Rochdale Hornets on Saturday 7 September 1895. Although the home side won 8-3, the campaign was not without its problems. They became the first team to be docked two championship points – for breaking transfer regulations by playing half-back Billy Jacques, even though he was still a registered player with Hull FC. The blue and whites eventually finished fourteenth out of twenty-two clubs. Joining the Northern Union rebels had also been a costly business. In June 1896, the Saints' committee announced a loss of nearly £150 for the financial year.

16

Tom Barton, the Saints' first-ever superstar, photographed in his England cap in 1906. A marvellous footballer, he could play with equal power and skill in almost any position in the backs. His generalship dominated a game, while his tackling and kicking were superb. According to one critic: 'He would leave a trail of dead and dying in his wake. Where he could not swerve or side-step, he went straight on, his great strength, speed and determination carrying him through all but the best defences.' Yet most of all, he could run. Over 120 yards, Barton was the fastest man for miles around. He won the professional championship at Leigh in 1910, sprinting 100 yards in just over 10 seconds. His feat was all the more remarkable as the race was open to all-comers from anywhere in the British Isles. Captain of the St Helens team which lost to powerful Huddersfield in the 1915 Challenge Cup final, Barton was a near-automatic selection for the first English touring team to Australia and New Zealand, five years before. Yet there is no record of his prowess down under. He did not make the trip because the Rugby League would not make up his wages to his mother while he was away. There were no allowances for single men. His name appeared on the official list and on several photographs of the party, but he never toured.

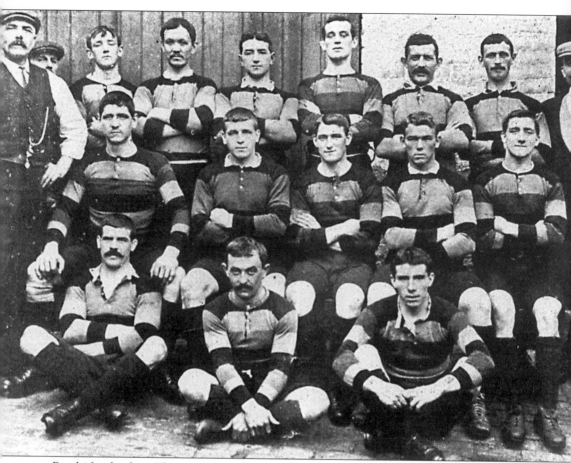

Ready for the fray. Thirteen red, amber and black hooped Saints and a reserve line up in the yard of the Talbot Hotel before the league match with Warrington on 28 September 1907. The home side won a magnificent game 7-6, one of only seven victories enjoyed by them during the 1907/08 season. Hillen scored a try and Charlie Creevey kicked two goals. From left to right, back row: Smith and Appleton (trainers); Matt Creevey, one of the fastest half-backs off the mark ever seen, a world champion standing jumper and 70 yards professional sprinter; W. Mercer, occasional pack member; Jim Mavitty, county forward, star swimmer and one of the strongest men ever to wear a Saints jersey; Jack Pope, towering hooker; Bill Whiteley (reserve), last of the original Cumbrian imports from the pre-Northern Union days; W.J. 'Gillie' Hillen, a Cumbrian centre; Sgt Major Hannaford (committee). Middle row: Frank Mooney, tough forward from the Pocket Nook district; Jim 'Butcher' Prescott, a rough and ready Lancashire County packman; Jimmy Creevey, skipper and centre three-quarter from the Pocket Nook Shamrocks; Charlie Creevey, the last of the three brothers who was strong, fast and a regular goal-kicker who later played for Wigan; J. Bate, understudy for regular winger Jack Manchester. Front row: William 'Kitty' Briers, a Thatto Heath lad and blacksmith's striker at Lea Green Colliery; Frank Drake, signed the previous week from Salford and set to debut at scrum-half; Teddy Toole, full-back or scrum-half, completes the Pocket Nook connection. The best dribbling forward the Saints ever had, William Briers made 512 appearances for St Helens from 1895 until 1912, a record beaten only by Bill Benyon and Kel Coslett in the 1970s.

Two
Recs Rivalry
1920-1940

St Helens RLFC in their Diamond Jubilee year in 1935/36, photographed outside the pavilion at Watersheddings, before a match against Oldham. From left to right, back row: C. Pennington (assistant trainer), G. Lewis (coach), T. Hall, A. Lemon, R. Atkin, D. Cotton, J. Bradbury, A. Owen (committee), J. Carson (trainer). Middle row: T. Holsgrove, A. Butler, W. Mercer (captain), I. Davies, O. Griffiths, P. Smith. Front row: C. Glover, H. Frodsham.

Charlie Crooks, Saints' full-back in the 1920s, in his Lancashire jersey. A local lad who had trials for Liverpool Football Club in his youth, Charlie's career was plagued by knee problems, which eventually forced his retirement in the early thirties. Although he never received international recognition, he scored a magnificent 'kick-and-chase' try for Lancashire against Yorkshire at Oldham in 1924 in the final minutes to seal a 6-5 success for the Red Rose County. Charlie maintained that preparations for the 1930 Challenge Cup final were thwarted by stink bombs and high jinks from certain players, which wrecked sleep patterns in their hotel on the eve of the match. According to Charlie, 'After finally getting back to bed for a few hours fitful sleep, breakfast turned out to be poached eggs as hard as bullets and toast like corrugated iron. No wonder we felt anything like confident when we trooped onto the Wembley turf.' Despite such disappointment, local newsagent Charlie remained a staunch St Helens fan – and a bachelor – for the rest of his life.

The Saints line-up for the 1925/26 season (players only). From left to right, back row: W. Clarey, Foster, P. Molyneux, E. Shaw, B. Briers, Fisher. Front row: A. Frodsham, W. Wright, C. Crooks, T. Flynn, G. Cotton, Woodward. Sitting: L. Fairclough, G. Lewis (captain), Lightfoot.

At a time when Britain was paralysed by the General Strike and J.L. Baird was inventing television, the Saints were developing a side which, at last, would be capable of challenging for major honours. The 1925/26 campaign – the club's jubilee season – saw a continued improvement in playing fortunes, with the team finishing in tenth position in the league, with 18 victories from 34 matches. Pacy wingman Walter Wright led the try-scorers with 19 touchdowns, while Welsh centre and captain George Lewis kicked 65 goals. Stand-off Leslie Fairclough, a rising star on the county and international fronts, helped to turn the Saints into one of the most attractive teams in the league before the end of the decade. Another vital cog in the future success of the Knowsley Road attacking machine was winger Alf Ellaby (right), who also made his debut during the 1925/26 campaign.

ELLABY'S BENEFIT

ALF ELLABY

SOUVENIR PROGRAMME

Saturday, Feb. 18th 1933

Testimonial programme for Saints' winger Alf Ellaby, arguably the club's first superstar, who could add an extra couple of thousand to the gate. Ellaby came into the game in remarkable circumstances. Born in St Helens, he had been a soccer player with Rotherham United until knee damage was thought to have ended his career prematurely, at the age of twenty-three. Yet the injury was cured by Recs' trainer Ted Forber and Ellaby began training with local rivals Saints. He was an immediate success with his devastating pace and handling ability. Most of all, he could score tries – 278 of them in 290 appearances for the Saints, a record later broken by Tom Van Vollenhoven. Alf was a regular for county and country and became a star down under after two Great Britain tours. Even though he was over six foot, he possessed such amazing flexibility that he could stoop when on the run and pick up a ball from the ground without stopping. In 1934, cash-strapped St Helens sold Ellaby to Wigan, where he enjoyed continued success. He returned to Knowsley Road for a short spell in the late 1930s, but was then past his best.

Alf Ellaby (right) with second rower Ben Halfpenny and stand-off Les Fairclough, stalwarts of the powerful Saints side of the late 1920s. All three were selected to tour Australia in 1928. Notice Halfpenny's distinctive headgear, essential in an era when scrummaging was such a vital part of the game.

St Helens RLFC Lancashire Cup winners in 1926, the team which brought the first major honour to Knowsley Road. From left to right, back row: Fred Smith (trainer), Mr Horsfall (referee), Lou Houghton, Ernie Shaw, Fred Roffey (captain), Bob Atkin, Bill Clarey, Fred Herbert (groundsman), Cuddy Pennington (assistant trainer). Middle row: Alf Ellaby, George Lewis, Charlie Crooks, Alf Frodsham, George Cotton, Albert Simm. Front row: Les Fairclough, B. Wilson (mascot), Walter Groves. The final against local rivals the Recs attracted enormous interest and over 19,000 packed into Wilderspool Stadium in Warrington to see the Saints triumph by 10-2. Ellaby and Fairclough scored a try each and Lewis kicked 2 goals.

Second rower Fred Roffey wears his Welsh jersey and cap for the photographer. Although born in Wales, Roffey spent his early youth in South Godstone in Surrey. He began his career with Wigan and won every honour in the game with the Riversiders before a dispute over pay saw him signing for St Helens in September 1925 at the age of thirty-two. As pack leader and captain, Roffey's undoubted experience was a big factor in the Saints' successful Lancashire Cup run. St Helens met the Recs again in the Championship semi-final at City Road on 24 April 1927 and the Recs exacted revenge with a 33-0 victory. The match was an ill-disciplined spectacle from the start with Groves and Houghton sent off for the Saints and Fred Roffey a limping passenger on the wing.

A cartoon from the St Helens newspaper, Friday 7 January 1927. The illustration not only features prominent players and officials from the Saints and the Recs, but also shows the tremendous rivalry and sheer interest in Rugby League which existed in the town in the mid-1920s, a veritable golden age. Although relative 'babes' in terms of their existence – they entered the league just after the First World War – the Recs won a major honour (the Lancashire Cup) before their Saintly opponents, in 1923. Unfortunately, the club was unable to sustain its remarkable early success. Money was not coming in through the gate as Pilkington employees gained admission virtually free with their recreation membership cards. The club eventually folded in 1939, although a thriving amateur organisation still exists today.

Second rower Albert Fildes, in his England jersey and cap as a St Helens Recs player. He formed a famous back-row partnership at City Road with team-mates Tommy Smith and Bill Mulvanney before his transfer to local rivals Saints, who had long been admirers of his prodigious tackling and work rate. Albert made 15 appearances for his country, mostly with the Recs, including selection for the 1928 and 1932 Australian tours. For the latter, Albert missed out on a Championship final appearance for the Saints against Huddersfield, on 7 May. Both Fildes and his team-mate Alf Ellaby, had already begun the long sea crossing to Australia.

A local product with great hands and a deceptive turn of pace, Bill Mercer secured a centre berth in the late 1920s and scored a try in the Saints' 22-10 victory over a powerful Wigan side in the 1930 Challenge Cup replay at Mather Lane, Leigh. Although the team was unsuccessful in the final, Mercer managed to pick up a Championship winner's medal in 1932 against Huddersfield at Belle Vue, Wakefield, where he played inside New Zealand winger Roy Hardgrave. Club captain during the Saints' Diamond Jubilee season in 1935/36, Mercer went on to give many years service as trainer/coach to the St Helens 'A' team and was able to keep an eagle eye on one of his most promising youngsters: Bill worked for the Corporation as a joiner, where one of his apprentices in the mid-1950s was a certain Alex Murphy.

One of the most famous victories from between the wars took place at Mather Lane, Leigh, on Wednesday 2 April 1930 when underdogs St Helens defeated rivals Wigan 22-10 in a replayed Challenge Cup semi-final tie in front of 24,000 spectators, a ground record. Tries were scored by Ellaby (2), Houghton and Mercer, and skipper George Lewis kicked 5 goals. Unfortunately, the Saints fell victim to a giant-killing act themselves in the final courtesy of the men from Widnes.

Above: St Helens defeated Huddersfield by 9-5 in the Championship final of 1932. Here, George Lewis is carried from the Belle Vue pitch by Jack Arkwright and Bob Atkin, with the coveted trophy safely in his grasp. *Below:* several team members line up for the photographer to celebrate Saints' first-ever Championship success. From left to right: Roy Hardgrave, Jack Garvey, Harry Frodsham, Tom Winnard, Bob Jones, George Lewis and Bob Atkin. Notice the mascot, complete with replica jersey and cap.

Tables of suggested Players Wages for Season 1936/37.

1st Team.

Home Win   £3. 5. 0   5/- increase.   3.15.0
      Loose £1. 10. 0   5/- less   2-10.0
Away Win Lancashire Clubs. £ 3. 15. 0   5/- increase.   4-0.0
      Loose   do   do   £ 1. 15. 0   5/- less.   2-10.0
Away Win Yorkshire or Barrow £ 4. 5. 0   5/- increase.   4-15.0
      Loose   do   do   £ 1. 15. 0   5/- less.   2.15.0

Reserves paid looseing money. Selected from, result of match.

A. Team.

Home Win.   £1. 15. 0   9. 0 less.
      Loose   £- 10. 0   9. 0 less
Away Win   £1. 2. 6   8. 6 less
      Loose   £- 12. 6   6. 6 less.

Juniors.
------- To be paid at   6. 6 for the first 6 matches. Win or loose.
         after   9. 0 for a loose and 14. 0 for a win.
         After playing with the First Team they come on higher rates.

Tea Money. Both Teams.
---------- ----------
         This will be allowed at the rate of 2/6 for all Clubs on away
         matches other than, Liverpool Stanley, Widnes, Wigan, Recs,
         Warrington and Leigh.
         . If meals are provided by the Club, the above is not allowed.

Compensation.

         1st Team, if married or have dependants.   £ 2.   5.   0
                   single.   £ 1. 17.   6
         A. Team. if married or have dependants   £ 1. 10.   0
                   single.   £ 1.   5.   0

International and County Terms.

         If a player is engaged in International match
         an gratuity of £8 will be made in a lump sum.

         If engaged in a County Match a gratuity of £5
         will be made in a lump sum.

NOTE. The above Terms will be operative until they are cancelled
       by the Committee, notice of same to be given.

Players' wages for the 1936/37 season were a far cry from the large pay packets earned by today's top stars at Knowsley Road. There does seem, however, to have been some alteration to the initial list of terms by the St Helens committee. Rugby League was a part-time sport: players were paid on a match-by-match basis and did not receive a weekly wage. Playing terms were agreed at the start of the season and each player signed a contract. Rates of pay varied according to the financial resources of the club. St Helens was not the richest of clubs at this time, although there was the usual financial incentive for coming back with two points from deepest Yorkshire and Barrow.

Three
The Sullivan Years
1952-1959

From 1921 to 1945 full-back Jim Sullivan dominated Wigan's all-time appearances, goals and points tables, going on to further success as coach of the Central Park outfit after the Second World War. Saints' chairman Harry Cook had no qualms about bringing this legendary figure to St Helens in the summer of 1952. It was a masterstroke and a move which helped to propel the St Helens club into the Rugby League elite.

Above: Jim Sullivan meets his players for the first time in the pavilion at Knowsley Road. From left to right: Vince Karalius, Alan Prescott, George Parr, George Parsons, Jim Stott, Stan McCormick, Reg Blakemore, George Langfield, Doug Greenall, Bill Bretherton, 'Todder' Dickinson, Jimmy Honey, Ray Cale, Jim Sullivan, Bill Whittaker. *Below:* the Sullivan effect began in earnest with a stunning 41-2 home victory over Widnes on August 23 1952. Flying winger Stan McCormick completes his hat-trick to the delight of the packed crowd.

Hard-running, second row forward George Parsons joined the Saints early in 1948 from Newport after a host of clubs had been vying for his signature. An integral member of the pack at the time of Jim Sullivan's arrival, George later recalled that Sully's finest asset was as a motivator: 'Jim Sullivan was a great psychologist. He brainwashed us into believing we were better than our opponents. In previous years, we would go to Wigan and very often outplay them for football, but they won the match. The first time we went with Jim Sullivan, he came to us individually and named our opponent in the Wigan team. He would tell you, "Now look – run straight at him, he's a coward." He told us how weak the other team was and before we ran onto the field, we thought we were playing a junior Rugby League team, not Wigan. Needless to say, we won the match.'

One reason why Jim Sullivan managed to turn around the fortunes of the St Helens club so quickly was that the nucleus of a great side was already there. His first signing, however, was a masterstroke. Welsh centre Glyn Moses cost a bargain £800 fee from Salford. Moses had become disillusioned with Rugby League and had returned home. It was Sullivan who literally led Moses out of the wilderness to begin a new career at Knowsley Road as a full-back. This was a typical example of the coach's intuitive judgement of football talent. Glyn's rock-solid defence and attacking flair contributed to a remarkable unbeaten sequence in the league during 1952/53. He played in every match from January onwards and still had not collected losing pay by the end of the campaign. The sizzling Saints finished in first place in the league table, won the Lancashire League Championship and established a Northern League record by winning 16 consecutive away matches.

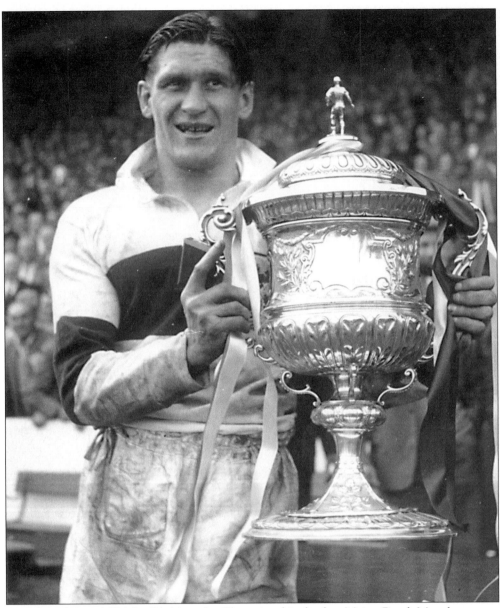

St Helens defeated Halifax 24-14 in the Championship final at Maine Road, Manchester, on Saturday 7 May 1953. Skipper Duggie Greenall shows off the gleaming trophy to the Saints' fans in the 51,000 crowd, the club's second Championship success. This did much to erase the defeat at Wembley against Huddersfield several weeks before. Three Welshmen got on the scoresheet: full-back Glyn Moses, loose forward Ray Cale and hooker Reg Blakemore, with a brace of touchdowns. Yet Man of the Match honours went to Thatto Heath-born stand-off Peter Metcalfe, who kicked 3 goals and scored a scintillating try. Several hours later, captain Greenall was parading the cup on the Town Hall steps and gave the huge crowd a rendition of his theme song, 'Mammy'. 'The boys want you to remember that this takes a lot more winning than the Wembley cup,' added chairman Harry Cook. 'It is the reward for a team's consistency throughout the season. I want you to pay your tribute with me to one man, the doyen of Rugby League, Jim Sullivan, and give him three cheers.'

The Saints show off the fruits of coach Jim Sullivan's first season in charge, the Lancashire League (left) and the League Championship trophy. The team were also beaten finalists in both the Lancashire Cup and Challenge Cup, a magnificent campaign by anyone's standards. Notice the traditional white St Helens jerseys, with the red chest and arm bands, a superb combination first introduced in 1925. From left to right, back row: Ray Cale, a loose forward from Welsh Rugby Union; Wilf Roach, a centre or wing and a local product; George Parsons, a second row from Welsh Rugby Union; Vince Karalius, loose forward and Widnes-born. Middle row: Alan Prescott, a Widnes-born front row signed from Halifax; Steve Llewellyn, right wing from Welsh Rugby Union; Bill Bretherton, second row and Wigan-born; Bill Whittaker, a front row signed from Widnes; Don Gullick, a centre from Welsh Rugby Union; George Parr, second row and a local product. Front row: Reg Blakemore, a hooker from Welsh Rugby Union; Peter Metcalfe, stand-off and local product; Stan McCormick, an Oldham-born winger signed from Belle Vue Rangers; Duggie Greenall, captain, centre and local product; Glyn Moses, a full-back signed from Salford; John 'Todder' Dickinson, stand-off and local product. Kneeling: George Langfield, a scrum-half signed from Castleford; Jimmy Honey, stand-off and local product.

The first St Helens team to win the Challenge Cup (in 1956) line up with the spoils at Knowsley Road. Left to right, back row: Duggie Greenall (right centre), Roy Robinson (second row), Nat Silcock (front row), Steve Llewellyn (right wing), Vince Karalius (loose forward), George Parsons (second row), Abe Terry (front row), Ray Senior (reserve). Front row: Len McIntyre (hooker), Bill Finnan (stand-off), Austin Rhodes (scrum-half), Alan Prescott (front row and captain), Jim Sullivan (coach), Glyn Moses (full-back), Frank Carlton (left wing), John 'Todder' Dickinson (reserve), Brian Howard (left centre). The final itself was initially

dominated by both packs, yet it was St Helens who began to open-out in the last quarter, with Frank Carlton scoring the all-important first try in the sixty-sixth minute. Further tries by Steve Llewellyn and skipper Alan Prescott, and two goals from Rhodes saw the Saints triumph by 13-2. Jim Sullivan was first on the field to hug his captain in triumph. For a few moments, both men wept joyfully until Sullivan turned away and headed back to the dressing room to let the spotlight fall on the players, which was the way he always preferred it.

St Helens defeat Bradford 53-6 in the Northern Challenge Cup quarter final on Saturday 24 March 1956. Second rower Nat Silcock's touchdown is ratified in dramatic fashion by referee Ron Gelder, much to the delight of hooker Frank McCabe. The two clubs had met six times in three successive seasons in the Challenge Cup in the early post-war years, with St Helens failing to register a single try in 480 minutes play. Retribution was swift this time, however, as the Saints ripped the visitors apart with a stunning 11-try performance, much to the satisfaction of coach Jim Sullivan and his famous 'no mercy' doctrine.

Welsh schoolmaster Steve Llewellyn, who took the Saints to Wembley in 1956 as a result of his magnificent solo try in the replayed semi-final against Barrow at Central Park, Wigan, on 11 April, in front of 45,000 enthralled spectators. The teams had cancelled each other out in the normal eighty minutes and the game went into extra time. In the eighty-ninth minute there seemed little danger as full-back Moses fired out a pass to Llewellyn 20 yards from his own line. He was faced by his opposite number, Castle, who seemed to have him covered, but who delayed his tackle. Llewellyn pushed him off balance and streaked away as the Barrow defence came across in vain. Finally, Castle caught his man 35 yards from the posts, but the tackle was high and ineffective. 'Llew' broke free, powered past scrum-half Harris and dived over the line to score without doubt the most important of his 240 tries in eleven years as a Saint.

Sully's record-breakers. The Saints were 1958/59 league champions with 1,005 points scored in 35 matches, the highest ever recorded in the league in one season. From left to right, back row: Dick Huddart, a hard-running second rower signed from Whitehaven during the season for £7,250, a record fee for a forward; Tom Grundy, prop forward signed from Blackpool Borough; Jan Prinsloo, former South African international winger and impossible to stop close to the line; Tom Van Vollenhoven, who finished the season with 62 touchdowns (breaking Alf Ellaby's former club record of 55) as the League's leading try-scorer; Abe Terry, a solid international prop with a deceptive turn of pace; Brian Briggs, a hard-tackling second rower from Wakefield Trinity; Peter Fearis, a goal-kicking centre, signed from Blackpool, who broke Peter Metcalfe's club record (of 145 goals from 1953/54) with 167 successes and also equalled George Lewis's thirty-five-year-old record of 13 goals in a match against Barrow on 14 February 1959; Walter Delves, loose forward and sometimes a hooker. Front row: Vince Karalius, loose forward supreme, just returned from the Australian tour where he was dubbed 'The Wild Bull of the Pampas'; Glyn Moses, full back, showing evidence of the knee injury which forced his retirement shortly afterwards; Alex Murphy, the world's greatest scrum-half and possessor of devastating pace and an astute football brain; Duggie Greenall, a stalwart of the post-war years and captain of the side, now the perfect centre partner for the devastating Tom Van Vollenhoven; Brian Howard, local lad and a fine utility back.

Local-born centre Ken Large scorches in to complete a sensational hat-trick of tries during the Saints' 42-4 thrashing of Oldham in the Championship semi-final at Knowsley Road on 2 May 1959. Large replaced the injured Tom Van Vollenhoven on the right wing for this match, but failed to make the line-up for the final against Hunslet at Odsal. As the match programme (below) shows, Vollenhoven played, though not fully fit, and scored three devastating tries which turned the match around for St Helens. Large was to gain ample consolation, however, partnering Vollenhoven in the centre during the 1961 Challenge Cup final against Wigan, a combination which produced one of the greatest tries ever seen at Wembley.

THE TEAMS

HUNSLET 22			ST. HELENS 44		
Myrtle, White and Flame Jerseys, White Shorts			White Jerseys with Red Band, White Shorts		
1 H. W. LANGTON 5 GOALS		Full Back	1 A. RHODES 10 GOALS	...	Full Back
2 R. COLIN ...	...	Wing Threequarter	2 T. VAN VOLLENHOVEN/K. LARGE	777	W. Three'qtr
3 J. STOCKDILL T	...	Centre Threequarter	3 D. GREENALL	...	Centre Threequarter
4 A. PREECE ...	...	Centre Threequarter	4 J. B. McGINN	...	Centre Threequarter
5 W. WALKER ...	...	Wing Threequarter	5 J. PRINSLOO T	...	Wing Threequarter
6 B. L. GABBITAS ...	...	... Out-half	6 W. SMITH TT	...	... ... Out-half
7 K. DOYLE ..T	...	.. .. Scrum-half	7 A. MURPHY TT	...	... ... Scrum-half
8 D. HATFIELD	...	Prop Forward	8 A. TERRY ...	...	... Prop Forward
9 S. SMITH ...	... ...	Hooker	9 T. McKINNEY ...	...	... Hooker
10 K. EYRE ...	...	Front Row Forward	10 A. PRESCOTT	...	Front Row Forward
11 H. POOLE T	...	Second Row Forward	11 B. BRIGGS ...	...	Second Row Forward
12 G. GUNNEY T	...	Second Row Forward	12 R. HUDDART T	...	Second Row Forward
14 B. SHAW ...	...	... Loose Forward	13 V. KARALIUS ...	...	Loose Forward

The Curtain Raiser being played before the game is between
BRADFORD LEAGUE Under 17 and KEIGHLEY LEAGUE Under 17

At the end of the game the Cup and Medals will be presented by
the Lord Mayor of Bradford (Alderman N. W. Durrant, J.P.)

Referee—G. WILSON, Dewsbury   Touch Judges—C. W. Allinson, Wakefield and W. E. Gibson, Warrington

A product of the famous Thatto Heath district, Austin Rhodes made his St Helens debut in the 1954/55 season and was an established member of the side when he appeared at Wembley against Halifax in the scrum-half berth twelve months later. He also gained fame in the full back position and was a key member of the 1957 and 1960 World Cup squads. A brilliant goal-kicker, Austin notched 10 goals in the 44-22 defeat of Hunslet in the 1959 Championship final at Odsal. His success was to continue after the Sullivan era with a second Challenge Cup winner's medal against deadly rivals Wigan in 1961. He also led the goal-kicking charts on two occasions, in 1959/60 and 1960/61. This superb all-round footballer later joined Leigh and Swinton before coming back to Knowsley Road for two seasons in the late 1960s. Austin's achievements were recognised with his induction into the Saints' Past Players Hall of Fame.

Tom Van Vollenhoven scores a fantastic seventy-five yard solo try against Hunslet in the 1959 Championship final at Odsal after beating no less than six defenders en route. Despite a nagging hamstring problem, the Van completed a memorable hat-trick. Team-mate Austin Rhodes revealed that the Flying Springbok had been a sensation right from the start of his Knowsley Road career: 'I remember the first training session when Jim Sullivan introduced him to us. We started doing some sprints and he was like lightning. We had a game of 'tick' rugby and he scooted in for four tries in quick succession. I said to Sully, "Good God, you've got a jewel here". He couldn't stop laughing, just like he had won the pools.'

Delighted Saints' coach Jim Sullivan celebrates in the Odsal dressing room after the 44-22 defeat of Hunslet in the 1959 Championship final, with Duggie Greenall (left) and Tom Van Vollenhoven. Sully had begun his reign at Knowsley Road in 1952/53 with the league title and was about to finish on the same high note. Several weeks later, the St Helens players paid a fitting tribute to their departing coach when Duggie Greenall presented Sullivan with a gold watch, inscribed 'To Sully, St Helens Players 1959'.

Hail the conquering hero. Chairman Harry Cook introduces three-try hero Tom Van Vollenhoven to the ecstatic crowd outside the town hall after the 1959 Championship success. Skipper Alan Prescott is on the left. Fellow prop Abe Terry draws on a cigarette with the mayor, Councillor Winter, poised by the microphone.

Four

Wembley:
Agony and Ecstasy

Saints' Wembley odyssey began in 1930 with the clash against Lancashire rivals Widnes, which was only the second Cup final to be played at the famous stadium. In those pre-motorway days, local travel company Ellison's organised their own special excursion. I doubt whether the starting time of 5.00 a.m. would appeal to today's motorway-orientated travellers.

The Saints of 1930 line up outside their gleaming motor coach in Victoria Square before setting out for special training at Buxton, with the Challenge Cup final against Widnes only days away. Big Jack Arkwright, fifth from the left, kicked his side to victory over local rivals Recs in the first round and was injured in the drawn semi-final against Wigan. He was controversially omitted from the final line-up and not allowed to travel with the team. Jack went down to Wembley, broken-hearted, on his motorbike.

The Saints might have impressed the cartoonist before the 1930 Cup final, yet some of their preparation left much to be desired. A tour of the Houses of Parliament on the eve of the match, courtesy of St Helens' MP Sir James Sexton, saw players return to their hotel at 1.00 a.m. Rumours of high jinks (including stink bombs) disrupting the chance of a good night's sleep came later as a jaded St Helens team lost 10-3 to unfancied Widnes the following day.

W. J. LINGARD,
PROPRIETOR.

NEW CROWN ST., HALIFAX.

.... 4th May 19 30

Dear Fairclough,

I wish to convey to you and your players my sympathy with you on your teams defeat Saty last at Wembley. The game itself was wonderful to watch and although you lost you had the satisfaction of knowing that you played "the game" and by so doing helped to lift up the R.L. game.

Sometimes defeat is hard to bear but a real sportsman who takes it in a proper spirit is worthy of high commendation.

Wishing both you, your players and Club future success.

Yrs very sincerely
Walter J. Lingard.

Some consolation for Saints' stand-off Les Fairclough after the 1930 Challenge Cup final disappointment against Widnes. The letter gives some idea of the esteem in which Fairclough was held throughout the Rugby League game, both at home and abroad. Some letters are not so complimentary, as Saints' Welsh winger Steve Llewellyn found out after a clash with Huddersfield's Johnny Hunter at Wembley in 1953.

On 25 April 1953 there was further disappointment for Saints' fans in the 89,544 crowd as St Helens went down 10-15 against Huddersfield. George Langfield is seen shaking hands with the special guest, His Grace the Duke of Norfolk. The former Castleford scrum-half notched seven points – a try and two goals – in what turned out to be a particularly bruising encounter, yet it was not enough to save the pre-match favourites from tasting defeat once again.

Wembley in 1953. Welsh flyer Steve Llewellyn crosses the line to bring St Helens back into the match at 5-5, just on the stroke of half-time, but it was to be to no avail. Llewellyn scored tries in both his Wembley appearances, in 1953 and 1956. Renowned for his spectacular swallow-dive finishes, he was to opt for a more orthodox approach at the famous stadium.

St Helens defeat Halifax 13-2 on 28 April 1956. The toast is to success as Precky and the boys savour the fruits of victory. From left to right: Glyn Moses, Brian Howard, Frank Carlton, Bill Finnan, Jim Sullivan (coach), Nat Silcock, Steve Llewellyn, Duggie Greenall, George Parsons, Alan Prescott (captain with cup), Len McIntyre, Vince Karalius, Roy Robinson, Austin Rhodes.

Many Saints' supporters kept copies of the match programme as a souvenir of their team's first Challenge Cup success. The fourteen-page publication cost one shilling and displayed the Empire Stadium in its original glory on the front cover (it was completely enclosed in 1963). The 79,341 spectators witnessed a bruising forward battle before left winger Frank Carlton broke the deadlock with a sixty-sixth minute touchdown. Rhodes converted and four minutes later another overlap on the right produced a try for Steve Llewellyn; Rhodes again kicked the goal. Skipper and Lance Todd Trophy winner, Alan Prescott, crowned a brilliant personal performance with an unconverted try almost on the final whistle.

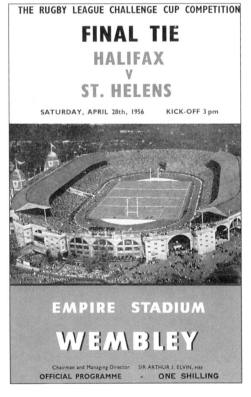

THE RUGBY LEAGUE CHALLENGE CUP COMPETITION

FINAL TIE
HALIFAX
v
ST. HELENS

SATURDAY, APRIL 28th, 1956   KICK-OFF 3 pm

EMPIRE STADIUM

WEMBLEY

Chairman and Managing Director   SIR ARTHUR J. ELVIN, MBE

OFFICIAL PROGRAMME   -   ONE SHILLING

Wembley in 1961, the year of the red 'V'. Skipper Vince Karalius and his team-mates are photographed with the Challenge Cup after the 12-6 defeat of Wigan. From left to right, back row: Don Vines, Mick Sullivan, Alex Murphy, Cliff Watson, Dick Huddart, Vince Karalius (captain), Bob Dagnall, Abe Terry. Front row: Tom Van Vollenhoven, Brian McGinn, Wilf Smith, Ken Large, Austin Rhodes.

The 1961 Challenge Cup final attracted huge interest, not just from supporters of the two teams, but also from neutrals. Rugby League secretary Bill Fallowfield's letter to the St Helens club confirms this. Interesting to see that the cup itself had to be returned for repair shortly afterwards. Shown at numerous events during the year by the winning club, it is inevitable that a little 'wear and tear' may ensue. Indeed, the Challenge Cup itself had been 'streamlined' by the late 1960s, with the removal of the neck below the lid.

THE RUGBY FOOTBALL LEAGUE

FOUNDED 1895

PATRON: HER MAJESTY THE QUEEN

PRESIDENT
THE RIGHT HONOURABLE
THE EARL OF DERBY

180, CHAPELTOWN ROAD
LEEDS, 7

SECRETARY
W. FALLOWFIELD, M.A.

TELEPHONE 4-4637/8
TELEGRAMS "NORFU," LEEDS 7

WF/MB

16th May, 1961.

The Secretary,
St. Helens R.L.F.C.
Knowsley Road,
ST. HELENS.

Dear Sir,

Congratulations on winning the Cup and on your teams fine display in what turned out to be a memorable Cup Final.

The number of tickets which each competing Club sold was higher than in any other year and helped to establish a capacity crowd for the first time in ten years.

When the excitement of having the Cup has died down a little will you please let me have it back in order to repair the damage which it sustained during the previous twelve months. The Cup has to be inspected by our Insurance Agents before being repaired.

Yours sincerely,

Secretary.

Sales.   St. Helens £4517.10.0
         Wigan   £4357.0.0
         HQ.   £5.223.7.0

Cartoon by Frank Barton in the *Liverpool Echo*. Notice the reference to the M1 motorway, which started to cut down journey times from the North to London considerably.

St Helens versus Wigan, 13 May 1961. Saints' South African wing sensation Tom Van Vollenhoven puts a foot in touch after a tackle by Wigan full-back Griffiths. Former Saint Frank Carlton is the Wigan player second from the right. In the sixty-third minute, with St Helens holding a slender 5-4 lead, came the deciding moment of this enthralling encounter. Second rower Dick Huddart pounced on a loose ball as a Wigan attack broke down ten yards from the St Helens line. Alex Murphy moved the ball wide to centre Ken Large, who beat two opponents with a sizzling burst of speed and passed to Vollenhoven just before halfway. The Springbok ace accelerated away from opposite number Carlton and, seeing his way blocked by full-back Griffiths, gave a return pass inside to the supporting Large. The Saints pair kept up a scorching pace along the touchline and as two red-shirted defenders raced across in a desperate attempt to cover, Large whipped the ball out to Vollenhoven once more, who streaked away to touch down between the posts – a magnificent display of controlled running and passing at speed, pure Wembley magic. An inspired Saints team never looked back, winning by 12-6.

St Helens 21-6 thrashing of Wigan on 21 May 1966. John Mantle, the former Welsh Rugby Union back rower, goes over for the first of St Helens' three tries against the Old Enemy. Tom Van Vollenhoven is the player in support. Further touchdowns by Len Killeen and live-wire scrum-half Tommy Bishop emphasised the Saints' total domination in front of a record crowd of 98,536. Receipts topped the £50,000 mark for the first time.

South African winger Len Killeen deservedly won the coveted Lance Todd Trophy in the 1966 final. He scored a total of 13 points in the match (5 goals and a try), yet it was his incredible kicking which took the eye. In the ninth minute, Wigan loose forward Harry Major was penalised for a play-the-ball offence. It was committed five yards inside the Saints' half and approximately six yards in from the right touchline. Killeen astounded the capacity crowd and millions watching on television by hammering the ball over sixty yards to its target – with plenty of room to spare. 'What can you do with goal-kicking like that, at Wembley mind you', gasped television commentator, Eddie Waring. It was the longest kick ever seen at the stadium and nothing was more guaranteed to spread total despondency in the Wigan ranks.

St Helens defeat of Leeds on 13 May 1972 by 16-13. Second rower Eric Chisnall, one of the finest home-grown forwards ever produced by the St Helens club, breaks through the Leeds defence before setting up winger Les Jones for a sixteenth minute try. Geoff Pimblett and skipper Kel Coslett are in support. Leeds winger John Atkinson is caught on the wrong foot.

Wembley, 1972. Saints' local-born scrum-half Jeff Heaton causes midfield mayhem in the Leeds defence. Eric Chisnall watches anxiously on the left, with loose forward and Lance Todd Trophy winner Kel Coslett in the background.

50

Sheer ecstasy as St Helens crush Widnes 20-5 on 8 May 1976. Saints' thirty-four-year-old prop forward John Mantle, replaced by Mel James in the closing minutes, reflects on a job well done. Notice the gloom on the Widnes bench behind him. This St Helens side was dubbed 'Dad's Army', with six players over thirty – Heaton, Benyon, Mantle, Coslett, Karalius and Nicholls. Indeed, the front row of Mantle, Tony Karalius and Coslett conceded thirty-one years to their opposite numbers, Nelson, Elwell and Wood. Widnes's youth was expected to tell in the soaring temperatures, yet this game proved the value of experience once again at Wembley. It was the Saints who finished the strongest, scoring three tries in the last quarter to seal a memorable triumph. Full-back Geoff Pimblett, with three conversions and two drop-goals, was a worthy recipient of the Lance Todd Trophy. 'Dad's Army' went on to a fabulous Premiership final success against Salford two weeks later.

Wembley, 1976. A fifth successive Challenge Cup final victory for the Saints. Skipper Kel Coslett, having received the trophy from Leader of the Opposition, Margaret Thatcher, is almost at the point of collapse in the dressing room with sheer exhaustion. 'Poor Kel was really dehydrated,' revealed team-mate Geoff Pimblett. 'I think he must have been playing on memory for the last quarter of the game. He had to be revived by a cold bath and salt tablets.' Youth did play a part, however, as twenty-year-old super-sub Peter Glynn notched two memorable touchdowns in the last six minutes of this pulsating encounter.

St Helens miss out at the Queen's Silver Jubilee Cup final on 13 May 1978, losing 12-14 to Leeds. Saints' hooker Graham Liptrot scores the opening try after four minutes Despite enjoying a 12-5 half-time advantage, the heavier Leeds pack gradually gained the ascendancy after the interval, although it took late drop-goals from Holmes and Ward to seal a Yorkshire victory in what is considered to be one of the great Wembley finals.

May 1987 and an attendance of 91,267 witness St Helens' narrow 18-19 defeat at the hands of Halifax. For the first time Wembley cup final receipts had topped £1 million. Saints' centre Mark Elia has the ball knocked from his grasp in a last-ditch tackle from Halifax loose forward John Pendlebury in the seventy-second minute as Halifax hung on grimly to their one point lead. A further Elia effort was disallowed three minutes later for a forward pass. Once again, the more experienced side had triumphed at Wembley. Coach Alex Murphy's young guns ignored the option of an equalising drop-goal to go all-out for the killer try which never came.

A disastrous day for St Helens rugby as they are crushed 27-0 by Wigan on 2 May 1989. Hooker Paul Groves halts the progress of Wigan's Tony Iro. Saints' Man of the Match Neil Holding (left) and Australian skipper Paul Vautin are also in the frame.

St Helens go down 8-13, again to bitter rivals Wigan, on 27 April 1991. Right winger Alan Hunte scores Saints' only try in the sixty-first minute, thwarting the attentions of Wigan's David Myers. Despite playing against a fatigued and injury ravaged side, St Helens made far too many handling errors and never truly extended their weary opponents. Scrum-half Paul Bishop, whose father Tommy played for the Saints in the 1966 final, completed the scoring with a conversion and penalty goal.

A disconsolate George Mann applauds the fans after the 1991 defeat against Wigan. The big New Zealand second rower was one of four overseas players in the red and white of St Helens that day. The others were Australian full-back Phil Veivers and fellow New Zealanders Tea Ropati and skipper Shane Cooper. This was the first instance of three Kiwis playing in a Challenge Cup final for St Helens since 1930, when Lou Hutt, Trevor Hall and Roy Hardgrave tasted defeat at the hands of Widnes.

Saints' haul of 40 points against Bradford Bulls at Wembley in 1996 was the highest score in a Challenge Cup final at the time, but was beaten only three years later by Leeds Rhinos 52-16 thrashing of London Broncos. Saints' third try of eight was scored after a powerful burst from winger Danny Arnold, despite a last-ditch tackle from Bradford's former Saints' second rower Sonny Nickle.

Some of Saints' 1997 Wembley squad assemble in front of the team bus at Knowsley Road, before heading south for the memorable back-to-back Challenge Cup success over the Bradford Bulls. From left to right, back row: Sullivan, Busby, Booth, Morley, Leathem, Anderson, Pickavance, Northey, Hunte, Haigh. Front row: Arnold, O'Neill, Matautia, Hayes, Martyn, McVey.

The killer blow, as Saints' second rower Chris Joynt screams over for his team's fourth try in the forty-eighth minute of the 1997 Centenary Challenge Cup final against Bradford Bulls. Stand-off Tommy Martyn is about to begin the celebrations. Goulding's conversion gave the team a virtually unassailable twelve points advantage. Another crucial four-pointer by stand-off Karl Hammond, just before half-time, had put St Helens ahead for the first time in the match.

Bringing it all back home. The victorious Saints squad show the cup to the crowds from the traditional open-topped bus, after their back-to-back success in 1997. From left to right: Derek McVey, Karl Hammond, Chris Joynt, Andy Haigh, Danny Arnold, Bobbie Goulding, Paul Newlove, Ian Pickavance, Kieron Cunningham, Steven Prescott, Anthony Sullivan, Chris Morley.

Five

Swinging Sixties and Sensational Seventies

George Nicholls (left) and Geoff Pimblett celebrate the Saints' 1996 Challenge Cup success twenty years after their own Challenge Cup and Premiership double with the club. Pimblett and Nicholls share the distinction of winning both the Harry Sunderland and Lance Todd Trophies. Signed from local Rugby Union in 1971, Geoff was a brilliant attacking full-back and goal-kicker, who developed a superb man-and-ball tackling technique. George Nicholls was one of the greatest second rowers in Rugby League history. Unstinting tackling, great handling skills and dynamic running power brought the former Widnesian 29 appearances for Great Britain, including two full Australian tours. Great players such as Nicholls and Pimblett symbolise the tremendous run of success enjoyed by the club in the sixties and seventies.

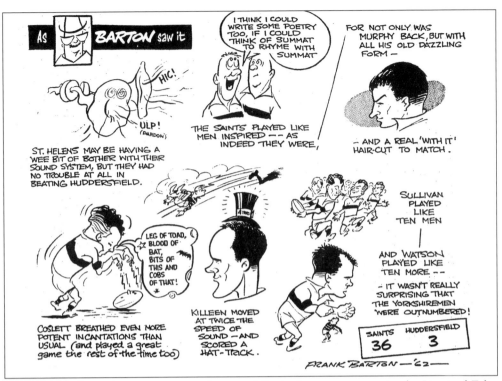

Above: Frank Barton's cartoons were a feature of Rugby League coverage in the *Liverpool Echo*, in the 1960s. Saints' crushing defeat of Huddersfield, which inspired the above masterpiece, was not matched when the two teams clashed a month later in the Challenge Cup at Knowsley Road. *Below:* A prostrate Tom Van Vollenhoven receives the magic sponge having copped a real 'bell-ringer' of a stiff-arm tackle from Huddersfield's Peter Ramsden. Referee Eric Clay and his touch judges are trying to sort out the melee, which involved both teams and a lone spectator. Both Ramsden and Saints' Alex Murphy were sent for an early bath, the latter for retaliation. The loss of Vollenhoven and Murphy was clearly a factor in the Saints' shock 13-2 demise.

Lancashire Cup kings. St Helens conquered Swinton 25-9 at Central Park, Wigan, on Saturday 11 November 1961. Skipper Vince Karalius shows off the trophy to the huge 30,000 crowd, with Dick Huddart taking the weight. Vollenhoven, Sullivan, Rhodes, Murphy and Large scored tries, with Rhodes kicking 5 goals. From right to left, back row: Fred Leyland, Dick Huddart, Bob Dagnall, Vince Karalius, Cliff Watson, Ray French, Wilf Smith. Front row: Brian McGinn, Alex Murphy, Ken Large, Mick Sullivan, Austin Rhodes and Tom Van Vollenhoven. Since the war the Saints have won the Lancashire Cup ten times and have been runners-up on seven occasions. Despite being losing finalists in 1958/59 and 1959/60, the club embarked upon a winning sequence of five finals on the trot from 1960/61 to 1964/65 – only one short of Wigan's record of six consecutive victories from 1946/47 to 1951/52. Remarkably, St Helens and Swinton monopolised those finals in the early 1960s. The two old rivals met each other for four seasons out of five, including three seasons in succession – 1960/61, 1961/62 and 1962/63. All the matches were played at Central Park and even though Swinton were one of the most powerful sides in the game at the time, they never managed to record a victory against their West Lancashire opponents.

The boys of 1966 display the silverware as the most successful team in the history of St Helens RLFC. Trophies on view include, from left to right: the Harry Sunderland Trophy won by Albert Halsall, League Leader's Trophy, Lancashire League, Challenge Cup, League Championship Trophy and the Lance Todd Trophy won by Len Killeen. Notice the classic 'red vee' jersey, adopted as first choice colours at the time. Skipper Alex Murphy, who was in dispute with the club, missed the photocall. From left to right, back row: Kel Coslett, loose

forward; Bill Sayer, hooker; Bob Dagnall, hooker; Cliff Watson, prop; John Warlow, second row; John Mantle, second row; Tony Barrow, centre; Jeff Hitchen, prop. Front row: Albert Halsall, prop; Billy Benyon, centre; Tommy Bishop, scrum-half; Frank Barrow, full-back; Tom Van Vollenhoven, wing; Ray French, second row; Peter Harvey, stand-off; Bob Prosser, scrum-half; Len Killeen, wing.

A stunning image from the St Helens versus Huddersfield league match at Knowsley Road on 24 November 1962. Full-back Kel Coslett, the Saints' new signing from Welsh Rugby Union, is about to convert one of the home side's 8 tries in a 36-3 success. Huddersfield players, Cherrington (11) and Haywood (4) wait for the inevitable. The highlight of the match was a stunning four-try display from South African wing Len Killeen. Tom Van Vollenhoven, seen walking back to his position, chipped in with a brace. Coslett was an immediate success in the thirteen-a-side code. An ever-present in his first season, he also led the goal-kicking charts with 156, a feat he equalled in the 1963/64 campaign with 138. Although his career was hampered by an ankle injury in the mid-1960s, when Len Killeen took over the kicking duties for a spell, he returned to top the charts once again in 1970/71 (183) and a phenomenal total of 214 goals and 452 points in 1971/72. Coslett created club records which are unlikely ever to be beaten given the number of games played in modern-day Super League. He also made the switch from full-back to loose forward with great aplomb, even turning out at prop in 1975/76. In terms of longevity, he is also unrivalled, making more appearances in the famous red and white jersey than any other St Helens player, with 519 from 1962-1976. A true Saints 'great'.

Alex Murphy, the greatest Rugby League player to come out of St Helens and one of the most well-known and respected players the game has ever produced, strikes again. Born in Thatto Heath and a member of the local St Austin's school side, he made his first team debut for Saints in 1956 and his blistering pace and astute football brain saw him go on to become the youngest-ever tourist down under in the Ashes-winning squad of 1958. He played in all the 1960 World Cup games for Great Britain and made 26 appearances for his country while at St Helens. A Wembley winner and try-scorer against Wigan in 1961, he also captained the Saints team which won four cups in 1966, including another Wembley victory over Wigan. He left the club somewhat acrimoniously after the four cups triumph, moving on to Leigh, but returned to coach St Helens from 1985 to 1990, including a Wembley appearance against Halifax in 1987. The award of the OBE in the 1999 New Year's Honours List was a most appropriate, if rather belated, reward for his services to Rugby League.

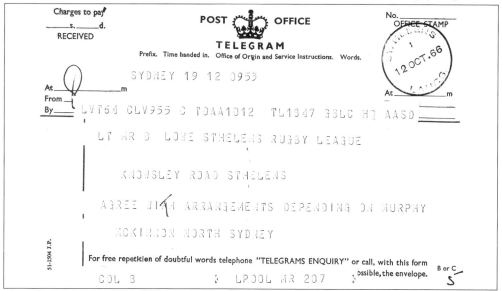

Unlike several Saints' players of his era, such as Len Killeen (Balmain), Mervyn Hicks (Canterbury), Dick Huddart (St George), Cliff Watson and Tommy Bishop (both Cronulla), Alex Murphy resisted the attraction of Australian club football, although as this telegraph reveals, North Sydney clearly hoped to add him to their roster in October 1966.

THE LEIGH FOOTBALL CLUB LTD.

AFFILIATED WITH THE RUGBY FOOTBALL LEAGUE
GROUND—" HILTON PARK," KIRKHALL LANE, LEIGH

DIRECTORS:

Chairman—MAJOR JACK RUBIN

Vice-Chairman K. FLETCHER, J.P.

J. B. HARDING, F.C.A.
C. H. COLLIER
J. S. ROBERTS
T. SALE
R. SHAW

All communications to the Secretary/Manager:
T. HOURIGAN, J.P., M.A.

Registered Office:
"HILTON PARK"
LEIGH, Lancs.

Telephone: LEIGH 71084
Secretary's Residence: LEIGH 73858

28th October, 1966.

TO THE PRESS:

My Board of Director were unanimous - rather
than let Alex Murphy go to Australia, I was empowered to offer
him a really wonderful five year Contract to remain with our
Club and really take us to the top.   Alex Murphy has seen
and agreed to the terms of the Contract and duly signed, and
was delighted to sign what we both think to be a wonderful
Contract.   What Australia can do; Lancashire, especially
Leigh, can do better !   Alex Murphy is staying with Leigh
and we are delighted, and we hope, as we both signed this
Press release, that our next and final stop is Wembley.

....
Chairman.

....
Team Manager/Coach.

Despite being the most successful captain in St Helens' history, with the four-trophy haul in 1965/66, Alex Murphy became involved in a dispute with the club about playing in the centre. He trained alone and the board put a £12,000 fee on his head. The world's greatest scrum-half was on the verge of signing a huge contract with Australian giants North Sydney before it was announced that Leigh had secured his services on contract at an agreed wage in the position of coach – clearly a reaction to the 'ridiculous and unrealistic' price put on his head. As long as he did not play for the East Lancashire club, the perplexed St Helens Board would receive absolutely nothing. The final chapter in the 'Murphy Affair' saw Leigh secure his playing registration after much wrangling for £6,000 twelve months later. On Wednesday 15 September 1967, Alex Murphy's first appearance as a Leigh player at St Helens caused traffic chaos as over 20,000 packed into Knowsley Road. This time, not even the Great Man's presence on the field was enough to prevent a crushing 22-0 defeat by the rampaging Saints. Love him or loathe him, you could never ignore him.

John Warlow was another fine example of the successful Saints' team-building policy in the early 1960s of signing players from a Rugby Union background. Taking the plunge in October 1963, John adapted himself well to the demands of Rugby League football, both in the second row and at prop. He soon became a dual international, making his first appearance for Great Britain against France in 1964. Warlow, together with team-mates Ray French and John Mantle, formed a huge back row during the successful 'four cups' season of 1965/66. John was selected for the 1968 World Cup squad, before moving to Widnes two years later. He returned for an Indian summer at Knowsley Road in 1972, however, helping the club to their one and only First Division title in 1975.

Frank Barton's 'Sketchbook'

No. 18: JOHN WARLOW (St. Helens)

Frank Barton's 'Sketchbook'

No. 16: JOHN TEMBEY (St. Helens)

Although the St Helens club bolstered their playing ranks with recruits from Rugby Union in the early 1960s, there were some key signings made from other League clubs. Prop John Tembey, signed from Whitehaven at the start of the 1962/63 campaign for a reputed £7,500 fee, followed his former team-mate Dick Huddart, to Knowsley Road and was seen as the replacement for local-born Abe Terry, who had joined Leeds for £8,000 several months before. Originally a centre who had switched to the second row before his graduation to prop, John was a superb footballer with the ability to offload the ball in the tackle. A Cumbrian county player, he also made two Great Britain appearances, against Australia in 1963 and France in 1964, before his transfer to Warrington early in the 1965/66 season.

St Helens crushed Oldham 30-2 in the Lancashire Cup final on Friday 25 October 1968 at Central Park, Wigan. Coach Cliff Evans and the boys begin the celebrations, having retained the trophy. The Saints would not win another County final for sixteen years. From left to right, back row: Myler, Coslett, Wilson, Benyon and Watson. Middle row: Rees, Sayer, Warlow, Rhodes and Chisnall. Front row: Bishop, Evans (coach), Whittle, Williams and Houghton.

St Helens triumphed 13-10 over Warrington in the Lancashire Cup final replay on Saturday 2 December 1967 at Station Road, Swinton. A proud moment for Tom Van Vollenhoven in his testimonial year, as he lifted a trophy for the first and only time as skipper of the side. Although the Flying Springbok signed off with a final appearance in a St Helens jersey at Hull KR in a first round play-off tie on 27 April 1968, his final appearance in England was at Thrum Hall, Halifax, on 3 May, when the Great Britain World Cup squad played Halifax in a warm-up match. Tom guested for the Great Britain team and 2,000 spectators saw him notch a parting hat-trick as Halifax were beaten by 25-2. Vollenhoven's testimonial cheque at the end of June was a record £2,800, a measure of his popularity amongst the fans.

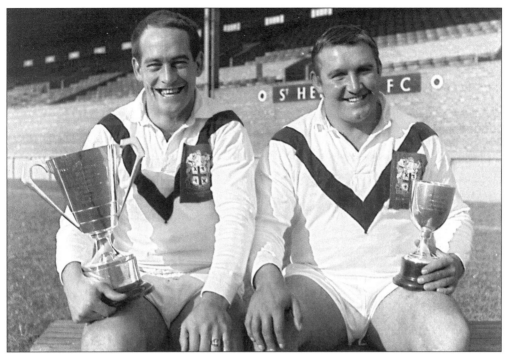

South African wing sensation Len Killeen (left) and barnstorming prop Albert Halsall display the fruits of the successful 1965/66 season. Killeen is seen holding the Lance Todd Trophy, awarded for his magnificent 5 goals and a try display in the Challenge Cup final against Wigan. Albert Halsall's Man of the Match performance in the Championship final against Halifax, included a hat-trick of tries, ironically the only three-pointers he had scored all season. Killeen also notched a hat-trick in the same match. The two former team-mates met up again at Knowsley Road some thirty-two years later. Needless to say the 1998 photograph brought memories flooding back.

Another St Helens triumph, this time by 24-12 over Leeds in the Championship final on Saturday 16 May 1970 at Odsal Stadium, Bradford. Saints skipper Cliff Watson holds the trophy aloft after a titanic struggle against their biggest rivals from Yorkshire. Despite trailing by 7-8 at half-time, the red and whites pulled away with a brace of tries from Eric Prescott (carrying Watson in the photograph) a loose forward playing as an emergency winger as a result of injury to regular number five Frank Wilson. Other points came from a try and 2 goals from John Walsh, 4 goals from Coslett and a three-pointer from hooker, Bill Sayer. The match was interrupted by torrential rain and a thunderstorm, with little cover for spectators in the huge Odsal bowl. Cliff was denied a second successive winner's medal twelve months later when a broken arm kept him out of the clash with Wigan.

B. Lowe Esq.,   24, Oakham Road,
Secretary,   Dudley,
St. Helen's Rugby
   Football Club,   Worcs.
St. Helen's
Lancashire.   4th July 1960

Dear Sir,
          In reply to your advertisement
in the Sporting Chronicle for
Rugby Football players, I offer
to you my services.

          I play Rugby Union
football for Dudley Kingswinford
as a second row forward and
played open side prop for
Worcestershire and Herefordshire
combined Counties last season.

          I am 20 years of age,
6' 3¾" tall and weigh 15st. 6lbs.

It pays to advertise. The search for big, powerful forwards knew no bounds during the summer of 1960 as the St Helens board took the unprecedented step of paying £400 for an advertising campaign in the national press, inviting top-class Rugby Union packmen to write to Knowsley Road for trials. Saints' initiative was rewarded with the signature of Cliff Watson, a solidly-built six-footer who had played in the second row for Dudley Kingswinford as well as representing Worcestershire and Herefordshire combined counties as a prop. Part of Watson's letter of application is shown here. London-born, Cliff soon earned first team recognition and went on to become one of the most formidable front row forwards of the 1960s, with 30 appearances for Great Britain. Although the Saints advertised for forwards once again in 1986, none of the applicants were invited to turn professional. Chances of unearthing a Cliff Watson were remote to say the least.

St Helens RLFC, First Division champions in 1974/75, the club's one and only success since the two division system was restored in 1973, and subsequently disbanded for the summer Super League competition in 1996. From left to right, back row: Eddie Cunningham, Eric Chisnall, John Mantle, George Nicholls, John Warlow, Tony Karalius, Roy Mathias, Frank Wilson. Front row: John Walsh, Jeff Heaton, Dave Hull, Kel Coslett (captain), Dave Eckersley, Les Jones, Geoff Pimblett.

A former Rugby Union player in his youth, Harry Cook (seen here with wife Ada) was headmaster at Rivington Evening School during the 1930s and soon began pushing promising youngsters in the direction of Knowsley Road. According to Harry, the Second World War meant an increasing involvement: 'As early as 1939 I was helping to pick the team, but during the war years there was a shortage of players. I trained a group of young RAF cadets and I would lend Saints as many as nine to make up a team. They kept the club alive during the war years.' Harry joined the board in 1945 and became chairman in 1950, a post he held until 1974, through some of the most successful years in the club's history, both on and off the field. Little wonder he was dubbed the 'Matt Busby of Rugby League'.

St Helens clinch a 16-12 victory over Wigan in the Championship final on Saturday 22 May 1971. This was the first time these old rivals had clashed in the final. In the dying seconds of a pulsating encounter, the Saints mounted one last attack. They trailed by just one point when John Walsh sliced an attempted drop-goal high and to the right of the Wigan posts. Centre Billy Benyon followed up at a cracking pace and caught the ball on the bounce before throwing himself over the line with Wigan's Stuart Wright powerless to stop him. Benyon, later dubbed the 'one armed bandit' as a result of a debilitating shoulder injury sustained earlier in the match, had turned what looked to be a certain Wigan victory into an unbelievable 16-12 Saints' success as Kel Coslett added a faultless conversion. Was he offside? Referee Lawrinson did not think so and that's all that mattered.

St Helens were victorious 32-20 over Warrington in the Premiership final on Saturday 28 May 1977. Celebration time for full-back Geoff Pimblett (left) and skipper Billy Benyon in the dressing rooms at Station Road, Swinton. It was a memorable occasion for Geoff Pimblett, who won the Harry Sunderland Trophy for his 7 goals and a try contribution – a Premiership final record at the time. He is one of a select band of players to have won the Man of the Match award in both Challenge Cup and Championship (Premiership) finals. It seemed fitting that Billy Benyon, in his twentieth major final as a Saint, should hold aloft the last trophy won by the club in the 1970s, such a glittering decade of success. Benyon's move to Warrington in October 1977, after sixteen glorious years with his home-town team, brought him the one medal missing from his collection, as he captained the Wires to an unexpected 9-4 victory over Widnes in the 1978 John Player Trophy final.

St Helens seal the Premiership final 15-2 over Salford on Saturday 22 May 1976. Saints' centre Peter Glynn dives over for a crucial sixty-ninth minute touchdown which helped to trigger off a points rush, after Salford had led by 1-0 at half-time. Glynn himself began the move in his own half with a neat pass which sent winger Roy Mathias on a scorching thirty-five yard run. John Mantle carried on the attack, before Glynn's fellow Widnesian team-mate George Nicholls (left) put him over with a superb reverse pass.

What would they be worth today? Members of the St Helens Challenge Cup and Championship double winning side from 1966 line up during the Saints' ground centenary celebrations in 1990. From left to right: Joe Coan (coach), Alex Murphy (captain), Frank Barrow, Peter Harvey, Albert Halsall, Ray French, John Warlow, Jeff Hitchen.

Centre John Walsh (right), seen here with Club President Lady Mavis Pilkington and television pundit Stuart Hall, was one of the most complete footballers ever to play for St Helens. A great goal-kicker who could drop goals with either foot, he possessed a fine sidestep and a crunching tackle. He went on to captain Lancashire and helped Great Britain to win the 1972 World Cup in France, producing a brilliant defensive display in the final against Australia. A World Cup member for England in 1975, he retired prematurely shortly afterwards, a sad loss on both the club and international fronts.

A sight which terrified opposing defences in the seventies; John Mantle makes another scything break, with referee Billy Thompson desperately trying to keep up. Notice the distinctive facial expression. An all-round athlete in his youth, John was signed from Newport RUFC in 1964 and became, arguably, the best forward ever to come out of Wales. A superb, hard-running and tackling second rower John made his Great Britain debut in 1966 and was an automatic selection for that year's Australian tour. A Wembley winner in 1966 and 1972, John switched to prop for the famous 'Dad's Army' final against Widnes in 1976. He made 420 full appearances for the Saints, scoring 68 tries before he joined Salford at the start of the 1976/77 season. A member of the St Helens Past Player's Hall of Fame, he is undoubtedly one of the greatest-ever back row forwards in Rugby League.

Six

Representative Rugby

The match programme from one of the most memorable matches in the history of Anglo-Australian football. Great Britain's walking wounded – including 'Captain Courageous' Alan Prescott, who stayed on the field with a broken arm – won the crucial Second Test at Brisbane by 25-18 and later went on to clinch the Ashes. Apart from Prescott himself, other Saints' players included Vince Karalius and a young genius at scrum-half called Alex Murphy. A stirring victory which will never be forgotten as long as the game is played.

The four Saints' players selected for the 1928 Australian tour. From left to right: winger Alf Ellaby, stand-off Les Fairclough, centre Alf Frodsham, second rower Ben Halfpenny. There were actually seven St Helens players selected – the other three, Oliver Dolan, Albert Fildes and Frank Bowen, were members of local rivals the Recs. This was an accurate reflection of a golden era for Rugby League football in the town which has seldom been equalled.

Saints' winger, Jimmy Flanagan, wears his red and white hooped Lancashire jersey in 1910. A pacy three-quarter who made six appearances for his county from 1909 to 1913, Flanagan also caught the eye of the international selectors, taking part in an Australian tour squad trial at Headingley with team-mate and second rower William 'Butcher' Prescott. Neither player was selected. The 1914 tour, famous for the 'Rorke's Drift' Test, when Britain beat the Australians 14-6 with only ten men, was co-managed by St Helens official Joe Houghton. As a result of an injury crisis, his son made a surprise appearance in an up-country match – even managing to score a try. How ironic that the first St Helens man to represent Great Britain on tour should be a comparatively second-rate amateur. Doubtless, Flanagan and Prescott greeted the news with somewhat mixed emotions. Unfortunately, Jimmy Flanagan was to lose his life in the First World War a few years later, one of three Saints' players to do so. The others were New Zealand full-back 'Jum' Turthill and Yorkshire centre Jimmy Greenwood.

Saints' prop forward Alan Prescott (back row, third right) and centre Duggie Greenall (extreme right) line up with the Great Britain squad before a training session at Hunslet, prior to the First Test against the Australians at Headingley 4 October 1952. Prescott made a winning debut in an Ashes Test as Great Britain cruised to a 19-6 success, in front of a near 35,000 crowd. Although Greenall was a reserve for this clash, he joined his club colleague in the starting line-up for the Second Test at Swinton and scored two tries in Great Britain's 21-5 victory which clinched the Ashes.

Forty years on. The Stones Bitter World Cup final featured Great Britain versus Australia on Saturday 24 October 1992. The St Helens and Great Britain centre and wing combination of Gary Connolly (left) and Alan Hunte look well prepared for the rigours of an Anglo-Australian clash, with matching thigh pads (or torpedoes) which were much in vogue at the time to prevent 'dead-leg' injuries. In a match totally dominated by both packs, it was Australia who secured victory with a try from centre Steve Renouf in the sixty-eighth minute. Saints' veteran prop Kevin Ward was also in the starting line-up for what turned out to be his farewell from the international arena at the age of thirty-five. The crowd of 73,631 at Wembley produced record receipts for an international fixture of £1,848,056.

Alan Prescott poses for the photographer with some of his vast array of honours from representative football, which included 28 Great Britain appearances, 12 for England and 14 for Lancashire. He became the first forward to captain a Great Britain touring squad and made two tours down under in 1954 and 1958, the latter as captain. Originally a winger with Halifax, Prescott joined the Saints as a loose forward and made the transition to the front row in the late 1940s, which was to bring him so much success for club and country. A born leader, Prescott was uncompromising (as front rowers had to be in those days) yet was considerably more mobile than most – a legacy of his days as a three-quarter. He was to find universal fame and acclaim for his part in the Second Test match at Brisbane on 5 July 1958. In the opening minutes Prescott broke his right arm, yet remained on the field to lead his side to victory over the Aussies and square the series. Having lost stand-off Dave Bolton with a broken collar bone and three other players badly hurt, Prescott carried on, defying the orders of the team doctor not to return to the fray after half-time. The British manager Tom Mitchell described his display as one of 'selfless sacrifice for his team and country, unequalled in any sport anywhere in the world. He gathered the ball, he ran, he dictated the pattern of play and he tackled well with his good arm. Only those present at the game had any idea of the man's naked courage.'

Great Britain defeated New Zealand 35-19 at Station Road, Swinton, on 4 November 1961. Club-mates Alex Murphy (left) and Mick Sullivan combine to bring down a Kiwi opponent. Quicksilver scrum-half, Murphy enjoyed a glittering international career from 1958 to 1966, including two Australasian tours. Chosen as the youngest-ever tourist in 1958, the hard pitches down under certainly suited his devastating pace. However, clashes with the game's hierarchy meant that he lost the chance of a third tour in 1966. Alex was later recalled into the Test arena as a Leigh player in 1971. A tough-tackling, hard running three-quarter, Mick Sullivan made 10 appearances for his country in his 3 seasons as a Saint, part of a record total of 46 overall in his career with his other clubs – Huddersfield, Wigan and York – a figure later equalled by the Hull and Leeds star Garry Schofield in the 1990s.

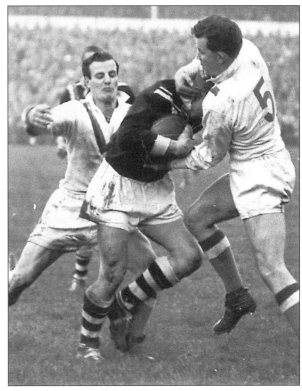

Great Britain defeated Australia 11-4 in the World Cup on 24 October 1970 at Headingley, Leeds. Great Britain prop Cliff Watson prepares to meet the challenge of Australian full-back Eric Simms. The home side, under the captaincy of Saints' Frank Myler, forced a play-off against their famous adversaries for World Cup glory. Unfortunately, hopes dashed in a brutal, brawling encounter, which Australia won 12-7. Two days later, at Knowsley Road, it was left to St Helens to show the acceptable face of British Rugby League with a sensational 37-10 victory over the newly-crowned world champions. The most capped prop forward of all time with 30 full and 1 substitute appearance in his 8-year international career, Watson was always a handful in Test matches. A member of the 1968 and 1970 World Cup squads, Watson also toured Australia in 1966 and 1970. Before leaving St Helens for Australian club Cronulla in 1971, Cliff was presented with a record £3,111 testimonial cheque, just reward for eleven years of stalwart service for club and country.

Great Britain slump to 3-11 against Australia at Station Road, Swinton on Saturday 9 December 1967. A real 'David and Goliath' situation, as St Helens and Great Britain scrum-half Tommy Bishop attempts a tackle on the giant Aussie second rower Elton Rasmussen. Other Great Britain players include stand-off Roger Millward and captain Bill Holliday. Scrum-half Billy Smith is the supporting Kangaroo. Played on a bone-hard pitch in Arctic conditions, the visitors became the first Australian team to retain the Ashes in England. Bishop proved to be a real thorn in the side of the Australians ever since his Ashes debut at the Sydney Cricket Ground in the successful First Test of 1966, and was not afraid of anyone in the green and gold jersey, regardless of size. He made 15 appearances in Test matches, before his transfer to the Sydney club Cronulla in 1969.

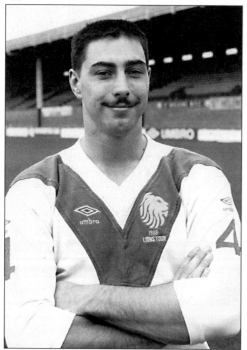

Saints' centre Paul Loughlin poses in his 1988 Australian tour jersey at Knowsley Road. A fine winger's centre and goal-kicker, Loughlin played at full-back in the first two Tests of the 1988 series. It was in the Third Test at the Sydney Cricket Ground, when Louglin was restored to his more accustomed role in the centres, that he made quite an impact. Apart from notching three vital goals, his jinking run just inside his own half and well-timed pass to Henderson Gill saw the Wigan winger dash forty yards for a crucial four-pointer, arguably the turning point in a surprise 26-12 victory for Great Britain's patched-up side. Loughlin made 14 full appearances for Great Britain, from 1988 to 1992, often with the Widnes and Wigan flyer Martin Offiah outside him.

Veteran prop Kevin Ward enjoyed a fabulous Indian summer at Knowsley Road in the early 1990s. Still a potent force, he is seen taking the ball up in typical fashion against Australia in the 1992 World Cup final. Wigan's Shaun Edwards and Deryck Fox of Bradford are also in shot.

Proud Saints' chairman Harry Cook presents international caps to Mike Sullivan, Dick Huddart and Alex Murphy before a match at Knowsley Road. They were key members of the Great Britain team which toured Australia and New Zealand in 1962.

Tormentors of the Australians on the 1958 tour. A young Vince Karalius (left) and Dick Huddart (below) seen in Test match action for Great Britain against France at Wigan in 1962. At 6 feet and 15 stone, Huddart's greatest asset was the ability to take a pass on the burst and carve a huge hole in the opposing defence with a devastating combination of speed and tearaway straight running. It took a record fee for a forward of £7,250 to bring the former Whitehaven man to Knowsley Road. His close pal Vince Karalius had terrified the Aussies with his bear-hug tackles and was dubbed the 'Wild Bull of the Pampas' by an adoring media. It is hard to believe that both were making their first appearance in an Anglo-Australian encounter in the crucial Second Test at Brisbane, which Great Britain won 25-18, against seemingly impossible odds. Dick was also a member of the 1962 Australian tour squad, which retained the Ashes in convincing fashion.

Arguably Saints' greatest-ever stand-off half, Leslie Fairclough terrorised opposing defences in the mid-1920s with his speed off the mark and superb handling skills. He is pictured (second left in the front row) with the Great Britain team which took on New Zealand in the Second Test at the Boulevard, Hull, on Saturday 13 November 1926. Fairclough scored a try in the home side's 21-11 success. Fairclough became the first St Helens player to captain Great Britain, against Australia, also at Hull on 5 October 1929.

Despite phenomenal success with the Saints in the 1970s – 216 tries from 412 appearances in just over a decade at Knowsley Road – Roy Mathias played just one Test match for Great Britain, against Australia in Brisbane on 16 June 1979. The visitors were on the end of a 35-0 hiding and Mathias did not play in the other two Tests in Sydney. Les Jones, his partner on the right flank in the St Helens team in the 1970s, was also a prodigious try-scorer with 284 touchdowns from 485 matches, yet he too made just one appearance in the Great Britain jersey, against New Zealand in 1971. Mathias won 20 Welsh caps from 1975 to 1981, the second highest total behind the great Jim Sullivan with 26. He did not have devastating pace, but his strong, direct-running style made him almost impossible to stop with the line in his sights.

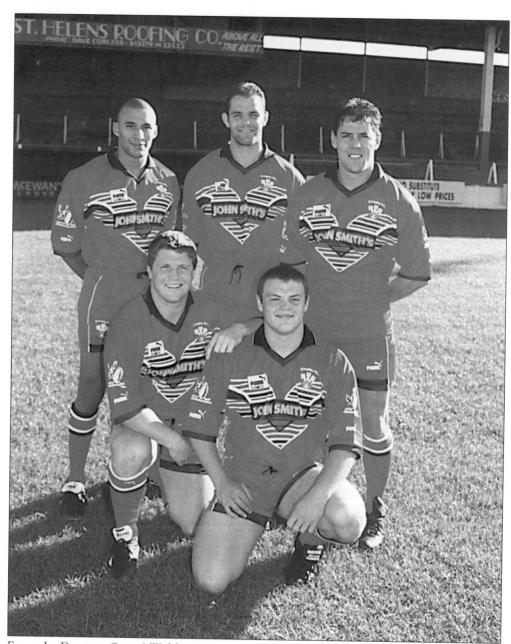

Enter the Dragons. Saints' Welsh contingent for the 1995 World Cup in full kit at Knowsley Road. From left to right, back row: Anthony Sullivan, winger; Dean Busby, second row; Jon Griffiths, half-back. Front row: Scott Gibbs, centre; Kieron Cunningham, hooker. Wales enjoyed a successful tournament, progressing through to the semi-final and a clash with England at Old Trafford. Gibbs, Sullivan and Cunningham took part in an entertaining encounter that was watched by over 30,000 fans. England's greater overall power saw them through 25-10 with tries from Offiah (two), Betts, Clarke and Newlove. The Welsh influence has been a feature at Knowsley Road since the late 1940s with names like Parsons, Llewellyn, Coslett and Warlow, although the flow of talent from the Valleys seemed to dry up in the late 1990s as a result of full-time professionalism in the fifteen-a-side code.

Seven
Overseas Connections

Saints' first-ever overseas signing, scrum-half Arthur Kelly, who joined the club following the inaugural British tour by New Zealand in 1907/08. As well as producing home-grown talent by the bucketful, the St Helens club has continued to look overseas for top-class stars in New Zealand, Australia, Western Samoa and South Africa. Indeed, it is that special mix of home-grown and imported talent which creates such interest on the terraces. Long may it continue.

So close. Saints' flamboyant South African-born winger Len Killeen makes a desperate and rather unorthodox attempt to score against the old enemy, Wigan, in front of an incredulous Popular Side at Knowsley Road on Good Friday in 1964. Killeen was very much the all-round sportsman. A renowned cricketer, he attended the same school as South African international Peter Pollock, represented his country at basketball and was a First League baseball player. He took over the Saints' kicking duties from the injured Kel Coslett in 1964/65 and became the only player to head both the try-scoring (32) and goal-kicking charts (120) twelve months later: a feat which may never be equalled. Len made 187 appearances for the Saints, scoring 115 tries and kicking 408 goals, a fine record. He left for Australia in 1967 and became one of a select band of players to have won both a Challenge Cup final and Australian Grand Final winner's medal, the latter for Balmain against South Sydney in 1969.

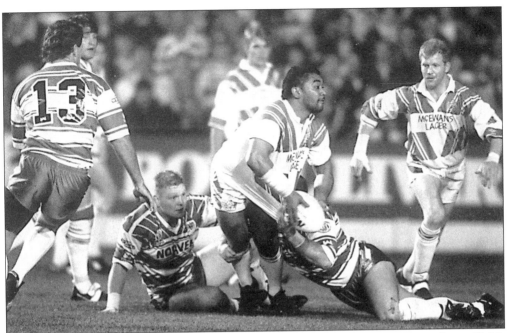

New Zealand front rower George Mann looks to offload during the Saints' magnificent 28-16 Lancashire Cup semi-final victory over Wigan at Knowsley Road on 10 October 1991. Hooker Paul Groves is on the right, with centre Gary Connolly in the background. George added mobility and penetration to an already formidable forward pack in the early 1990s. Other New Zealanders wearing St Helens' colours at the time were stand-off Tea Ropati and loose forward and captain Shane Cooper. The coach was former Kiwi international full-back Mike McClennan.

Australian superstar Mal Meninga makes his debut for St Helens in the 30-16 defeat of Castleford on Sunday 7 October 1984. There were good times on the horizon, including Lancashire Cup success over Wigan and an exhilarating 36-16 victory over Hull KR in the Premiership final at Elland Road, with Meninga himself chipping in with two brilliant interception tries.

Brett Clark, a lively half-back from the Western Suburbs club in Sydney who joined the Saints for the 1986/87 campaign. A capable defender who was more than adept at tackling, Clark was also a great finisher, with 19 tries from 36 appearances in a season which promised so much yet ended in disappointment with defeat by unfancied Halifax in the Challenge Cup final at Wembley. Clark was one of three Australians on the books during the campaign – the others were prop Pat Jarvis from St George and full-back Phil Veivers from the Souths club in Brisbane. New Zealand centre three-quarter Mark Elia completed the overseas connection at Knowsley Road. Clark went on to play for Oldham before finishing his career with Rochdale Hornets in the early 1990s.

Saints' Australian full-back Phil Veivers executes a copybook tackle to bring down a Barrow attacker in the Lancashire Cup-tie at Craven Park on 13 September 1992. Bernard Dwyer (left) and Sonny Nickle are also in the frame. A supposed 'makeweight' in the deal which brought Mal Meninga to the club in 1984, Phil almost became part of the furniture at Knowsley Road for the next decade. A real crowd-pleaser, blessed with great hands and an astute football brain, Phil ended up playing in a number of positions for the club, especially in the latter stages of his career, including hooker. Phil made 328 full appearances, with 96 tries, before enjoying a richly deserved testimonial in 1994/95.

Saturday 26 October 1957. The first of many for Saints' greatest-ever overseas signing, South African winger Tom Van Vollenhoven, as he scorches in for a try on his home debut against Leeds at Knowsley Road. Other St Helens players in the picture are, from left to right: stand-off Ray Price, Tom's centre partner Duggie Greenall, Walter Delves, Alex Murphy. Notice Tom's head leaning to one side in characteristic fashion, which usually meant he was in full flight, with a try usually the inevitable result.

Thanks for a job well done. Ten years on, Saints' chairman Harry Cook presents Tom Van Vollenhoven with a record testimonial cheque for £2,800 at the end of the 1967/68 season, his last before retirement. Tom scored 392 tries in 409 appearances for St Helens, making him the club's all-time leading scorer. His signing in 1957 triggered a number of South African signings into Rugby League, but there was no-one to touch The Van.

Two Saints' greats meet outside the dressing rooms at Knowsley Road in the late 1950s. Alf Ellaby (left), a star between the wars, appears to be giving some advice to Springbok sensation Tom Van Vollenhoven. It was the South African who broke Ellaby's try-scoring record of 50 touchdowns for a season, with 62 in 1958/59. Ellaby was a late starter in Rugby League, making 289 appearances and scoring 280 tries, Vollenhoven scored 392 from 409 appearances in his ten-season career. He is Saints' leading try-scorer overall, followed by local lad Les Jones with 284 and Ellaby. Although Ellaby was renowned for his pace and ability to hold even the most awkward of passes, Vollenhoven was also a rugged defender and a supreme cover tackler.

New Zealand international centre Jarrod McCracken is about to dump Leeds' prop Steve Molloy onto the Knowsley Road turf. A superb tackler, Jarrod was a real crowd-pleaser during his stay at St Helens for most of the 1992/93 campaign, when the Saints vied with Wigan for the First Division title, only to lose on points difference.

St Helens triumph 27-26 against New Zealand on Sunday 1 October 1989. Saints' second rower Paul Forber is about to send Kiwi winger Mark Elia sprawling onto the turf. Paul Groves awaits the outcome with interest. This was one of the most exciting games ever seen at Knowsley Road. St Helens, with very much a makeshift side as a result of injury, trailed 15-26 to the powerful Kiwis by three-quarter time, including a brace of touchdowns from Elia. In a dramatic finish, however, the home side staged a magnificent fightback to snatch victory with a Paul Forber try two minutes from time. Other try-scorers for the Saints were Alan Hunte, Dave Tanner and former Welsh Rugby Union international prop Stuart Evans. The crowd, mirroring the Saints' lack of form at the time, was a disappointing 7,040. Normally a centre, Mark Elia also had two spells as a player at Knowsley Road, taking a pivotal role in the 1987 Challenge Cup final against Halifax when the ball was knocked out of his grasp by opposition loose forward John Pendlebury just as he was about to touchdown for a crucial try. Elia's partner in the New Zealand team during the defeat at Knowsley Road was Kevin Iro, who became a Saint himself for the 1999 Super League season.

A Saints' signing for the 1988/89 campaign, Paul 'Fatty' Vautin, the Australian international back-row forward, was a whole-hearted competitor who endeared himself to the Knowsley Road faithful with a series of gutsy displays. The Manly stalwart was brought back for the Challenge Cup final clash against Wigan at Wembley in 1989, together with Michael O'Connor, and was appointed captain by coach Alex Murphy. Unfortunately, the Saints suffered a terrible hammering and 'Fatty' faced the wrath of his coach after disregarding his instructions to take a pot at goal in the last quarter of the match and kicked for touch with the Saints 17-0 down. The stigma of being 'nilled' at Wembley was obviously too much to bear.

Two reasons why the Saints were such a potent attacking force in the 1984/85 season. Aussie superstar centre Mal Meninga (left) and home-grown flying winger Barrie Ledger line up for the cameras before the 1985 tour of New Zealand by the St Helens club. Notice the special sponsored shirts by Pilkington. Meninga scored 28 tries and Ledger 30, with another Saint, Sean Day, leading the goal-kicking charts with 157. Heady days indeed.

A former New Zealand international half-back, Shane Cooper joined the Saints from the Mangere East club in the 1987/88 season. Astute and skilful with brilliant handling skills, he captained the club to success in the John Player Trophy, Premiership and Lancashire Cup competitions, together with two Wembley appearances in 1989 and 1991. His lightning football brain more than made up for his lack of pace. In fact, 'Merlin the Wizard' once scored six tries in a match for the Saints against Hull, a feat matched in St Helens' history only by flying wingers Ellaby, Llewellyn and Van Vollenhoven. He was an integral member of the team until the end of the 1994/95 season, when he joined Widnes. Shane made 269 appearances for the Knowsley Road club, scoring 76 tries. He was an all-time great.

St Helens versus Paris St Germain in 1996. Australian second rower Derek McVey storms over for one of his two tries in Saints' 52-10 success. Signed from Sydney club Balmain Tigers in March 1996, Derek missed the Challenge Cup deadline and a Wembley place against Bradford Bulls. The big Aussie made it to the famous stadium twelve months later, however, for the Saints' second successive victory, but it was touch and go. An ankle injury in a Super League match against Wigan at Central Park almost put him out of the reckoning. He became the first Australian to play in a St Helens Challenge Cup winning side. A powerful running forward with the ability to offload, Derek formed an impressive second row spearhead with skipper Chris Joynt which was used to great effect by the Knowsley Road club. McVey returned to Australia at the end of Super League II to play in the Newcastle competition.

A big crowd favourite, Western Samoan Fereti 'Freddie' Tuilagi spent much of his Rugby League career as a winger with Halifax until his arrival at Knowsley Road for the start of Super League IV. Switched to the second row by coach Ellery Hanley, his great power and athleticism gave another dimension to a side which finished the 1999 campaign with victory over Bradford Bulls in the Grand Final at Old Trafford. Freddie's spontaneous dance of joy at the final whistle will live long in the memory of Saints' supporters. The souvenir shop even stocked supplies of Freddie wigs, such was his popularity.

Eight
Field of Dreams –
Knowsley Road
1890-2000

Ode to joy. Loose forward Walter Delves scores against Featherstone Rovers on 23 August 1958, one of seven tries in the Saints' 32-9 success and a fine way to christen the new Main Stand opened by Sir Harry Pilkington before the match. This superb action shot by Bert Coulthurst of the *News Chronicle* and *Daily Dispatch* won the prestigious Sports Photograph of the Year Competition that same year. Someone who always seemed to enjoy his rugby, utility forward Walter was eventually transferred to Barrow after five years at St Helens during which time he made 102 appearances and scored 22 tries.

Jesse Skepper, the man who formed the Saints' Supporter's Club in 1923. He originally wanted to erect some form of shelter for stalwarts on the Popular Side. The first committee meeting was held in his front parlour in Spray Street, where he had a laundry business. The club began to hold meetings in the White Lion in Church Street and several of the game's notabilities, such as Lance Todd, came down to address meetings. Subscriptions were one shilling and the first financial statement at the end of 1924/25 revealed an income of nearly £600. Skepper's dream of a Popular Side stand became reality when the structure was finally completed in December 1925. Ever since its inception all those years ago, the Supporters' Club has continued to play a large part in making Knowsley Road one of the best-appointed stadiums in Rugby League, a marvellous testimony to the enterprise and dedication of men like Jesse Skepper.

A stunning fifties scenario. South African winger Jan Prinsloo finishes with a flourish during the 35-8 demolition of Dewsbury in a Challenge Cup-tie on 7 March 1959 at a packed Knowsley Road. Notice the open terrace on the Dunriding Lane End, now occupied by executive boxes. The scoreboard stands proudly in the corner with Skepper's Popular Side stand just in view on the right.

St Helens chairman Jim May presents skipper Fred Roffey with his Welsh cap before the home game against Widnes on 4 September 1926. The new Popular Side stand is in the background. The brainchild of Supporter's Club secretary Jesse Skepper in 1925, the structure was 220 feet in length and held nearly 2,000 spectators. The cost was a staggering £1,063. The current enclosure on the Popular Side was completed in 1962, with the old stand handed over to Liverpool City for their ground at Knotty Ash.

Tiger on the prowl. Dick Huddart makes a break against Widnes in 1959 with the old Popular Side stand as a backdrop. Peter Fearis is the player in support on the right. A sensational signing from Whitehaven in October 1958 for £7,250, a record fee for a forward, Dick formed part of a potent back row, which included Yorkshireman Brian Briggs and loose forward supreme Vince Karalius. After 209 appearances and 76 tries for the St Helens club, Huddart joined the St George club in Sydney for £10,000, a huge transfer fee at the time.

At the double. The Saints line up in front of the pavilion with the League Championship and Lancashire League trophies at the end of the 1931/32 season. From left to right, back row: F. Jones (chairman), S. Morris (vice-chairman), T. Winnard, J. Garvey, J. Arkwright, B. Halfpenny, E. Hill, R. Atkin, J. Houghton (treasurer). Front row: R.E. Jones, H. Frodsham, W. Groves, G. Lewis (captain), W. Mercer, R. Hardgrave, J. Marsh. There is a lack of terracing on both sides of the pavilion, together with the rather primitive player's entrance. Notice also

the long end-of-season grass. The Saints finished five points ahead of nearest rivals Salford in the Lancashire League competition and second in the Northern Rugby League behind Huddersfield, who were defeated 9-5 in the Championship final at Wakefield. New Zealand winger Roy Hardgrave led the club try-scoring charts with 44. Alf Ellaby scored 35 before his early departure on the Great Britain tour to Australia, the reason for his absence on the photograph.

Going public. Saints' first game as a Limited Liability Company, against Widnes on Saturday 28 August 1937. St Helens beat the Chemics in this traditional early season opener by 11-7. The attendance was 4,000 and the receipts totalled £138. Jackie Bradbury is the Saints' player being tackled, with Ted Beesley behind him. Note the unusual St Helens jerseys – a gift from the Supporters Club – and the original scoreboard in the background. A wooden fence ringed the playing area, replaced by the more substantial concrete version in 1946. The terraces behind the goal were nothing more than cinder banks.

Skipper Alan Prescott leads out his team from the famous players' tunnel at the Dunriding Lane End, which links the pavilion dressing rooms to the playing arena. A youthful Alex Murphy is close behind. Notice the Saints' change strip of light blue jerseys. The construction of new first team dressing rooms in the mid-1990s under the main stand has made the tunnel virtually redundant. What a thrill it was to see the Saints come out of this concrete abyss to the tune of 'Entry of the Gladiators' in the late fifties and sixties.

A rare action shot from a St Helens versus St Helens Recs match; the Lancashire Cup-tie at Knowsley Road on 23 September 1936. Saints' Arthur Cross is grounded by Howard and Jennion of the Recs. Notice the end of the Popular Side stand and the huge billboard – reputed to be the world's biggest – running the length of the Edington 'Kop' End.

St Helens versus Warrington, looking towards the Pavilion End on 30 April 1966, a view dominated by the gas-holder and electricity pylon. Notice the flagpole at the back of the terrace. This section of the ground is now occupied by the restaurant opened in 1973. Loose forward Kel Coslett waits to give Tommy Bishop (left) the ball for the scrum feed. The Saints won this top sixteen play-off match 35-7.

The new pavilion forms an impressive, though rather isolated, backdrop for the St Helens schoolboys, in training for a trailblazing fourteen-day visit to France in 1935. Funded jointly by the code's governing body, local business concerns and the St Helens Schoolboy Committee, the squad played matches in Toulouse, Villeneuve, Bordeaux, Biarritz, Bayonne and Paris, creating an excellent impression in terms of playing standards and behaviour.

Murphy's Men. The Saints line up in front of a much-changed pavilion before Alex Murphy's first match as coach, against Dewsbury in a John Player first round cup-tie on 24 November 1985. From left to right, back row: E. Leach (kit), S. Allen, G. Liptrot, B. French, T. Burke, P. Gorley, P. Veivers, C. Arkwright, G. Greinke, Alex Murphy (coach). Front row: R. Haggerty, N. Holding, A. Platt, B. Ledger, H. Pinner (captain), K. Meadows, S. Peters.

Battling against the elements. An unusual way of thawing out a frost-bound pitch as braziers are tried at Knowsley Road in early February 1956 in a desperate attempt to get the pitch ready for a first round Challenge Cup-tie twenty-four hours later against Warrington. The unusual methods paid off and the tie went ahead with the Saints winning 15-6, the first step on their way to eventual Wembley success.

Sheer ecstasy. Anthony Sullivan congratulates fellow winger Les Quirk on his touchdown which brought up a century of points against Trafford Borough on 15 September 1991. The Saints won a one-sided contest 104-0 and became the only professional team to score over 100 points twice in competitive matches, following on from their 112-0 scalping of Carlisle in 1986.

Castleford's international centre Arthur Atkinson, who entered the record books during the 20-10 success over St Helens on Saturday 26 October 1930. Despite a shock defeat for the home side against the unfancied Yorkshire outfit, spectators were amazed by his goal-kicking prowess, aided and abetted by a gale-force wind. Arthur Atkinson used the freak conditions to great effect. Following an infringement by Saints' second-rower Ben Halfpenny just after half-time, he placed the ball on his own twenty-five yard line and booted the leather between the posts at the Pavilion End. At over seventy-five yards this was the longest goal ever seen at Knowsley Road and a record unlikely to be beaten. 'I had only one grievance against this Castleford marvel', wrote one correspondent, 'that he did not attempt to kick a goal from the front of his own posts, the form he was in and the assisting wind made me inclined to believe that he would have succeeded.'

Saints' Rhodesian winger Len Killeen, the great all-rounder, boots over a conversion in the first round of the top sixteen play-offs on Saturday 30 April 1966. The Popular Side is packed near to capacity, part of a 13,500 crowd. Notice the unsightly graffiti on the back wall of the enclosure, relating to Killeen himself but now painted over. Lenny finished the campaign with 32 tries and 120 goals, the only player to have topped both the goal-kicking and try-scoring charts in the same season. On Saturday 7 November 1964, Killeen scored the longest try ever seen at Knowsley Road against the same opponents. Picking up a kick from Warrington's Geoff Bootle in-goal, he jinked and darted through the gap in front of him. Although chased by scrum-half Gordon, he touched down to the right of the posts, totally exhausted. Alex Murphy had to take the goal-kick as Killeen came back to a thunderous reception from the fans.

St. Helens Rugby Football Club.

GROUND—KNOWSLEY ROAD.

PATRON—THE RIGHT HON. THE EARL OF DERBY, P.C., G.C.V.O.

TELEPHONES: 716—HON. SEC.
697—GROUND.

HON. SECRETARY—HARRY INCE,
35, SHAW STREET,
ST. HELENS

13th Nov. 1925.

AT A JOINT MEETING WITH THE SUPPORTERS' CLUB COMMITTEE held in the GROUND PAVILION, on Wednesday, 7th Oct., 1925, the following RESOLUTIONS WERE PASSED: re "STAND".

COPY.

RESOLUTION. "That the first erection be a "Stand" 50 yards long, by 16 feet deep. Ground Committee & supporters' Club Committee to arrange for elevation etc.. .

RESOLUTION. "That a charge of 3d be made for entrance, which shall be taken by the Football Club Committee's Treasurer, and placed in a separate fund named "STAND REDEMPTION FUND", into which also the Supporters' Club Cash Balances, from time to time, will be paid, until sufficient is raised to clear cost."

RESOLUTION. "That the Chairman & Treasurer of the Supporters' Club, and the Chairman & Treasurer of the Football Club, jointly sign Cheques for withdrawals from the Fund, for payment of any charges against Stand erection.

It was agreed that the erection of Stand should be commenced fothwith, it being understood the Supporters' Club Cash Balance of £250 be at once paid into the fund named.

The above is a true copy of Resolutions passed at the meeting, and recorded in the Minute Book of the St.Helens R.F.C.

Yours faithfully,

H.Ince.

The beginning of ground improvements at Knowsley Road. Jesse Skepper's Supporters Club Committee met with officials of the parent club and a plan of action formulated as to when work on the new Popular Side stand would begin. This had been the main project in Skepper's mind when he formed the Supporters Club in 1923. Details of a separate account for the payment of construction work, the Stand Redemption Fund, were announced, into which the Supporters' Club immediately donated £250.

Come fly with me. Welsh winger Steve Llewellyn scores one of Saints' nine tries against Huddersfield in the Championship semi-final on Saturday 3 May 1953. The 46-0 success avenged their Wembley defeat seven days before by the Yorkshiremen. St Helens went on to beat Halifax in the final. Notice the packed Edington Stand in the background.

The changing face of the Pavilion End in summer 1989. The old scoreboard is about to be partially eclipsed by the construction of nine executive boxes and an electronic scoreboard. Completed in 1955, the original scoreboard became a police control room before its demolition in 1998.

A day to remember. Saints versus Wigan on Boxing Day in 1920. Local dignitaries and club officials, together with the imposing figure of Lord Derby, are photographed at Knowsley Road prior to the opening of the new pavilion. Charlie Crooks, Saints' captain, is pictured second right. The home team wore Lord Derby's racing colours of white shirts and black shorts for this particular match. Wigan stuck to their traditional cherry and white hoops, and ruined the party with a resounding 22-4 victory in front of a record 24,000 spectators. Prior to its construction, both teams had to get changed at a local hostelry – the Talbot Hotel in Duke Street – and rode to Knowsley Road on a horse-drawn wagonette. A description of the new building appeared in the St Helens newspaper at the time: 'In its rather isolated position, the building looks rather small from the outside, but a tour inside reveals it as a splendidly built and commodious establishment. There is an excellent gymnasium for the players, a beautiful bath, four feet deep and lined with white glazed tiles, thirteen feet long and ten feet wide – the most capacious in the Northern Union. There is a committee room, shower bath and offices. In short, it is a perfectly fitted and well-equipped football club headquarters and will be the envy of every visiting club from Lancashire and Yorkshire.' Despite an extension to create a sponsors' lounge in the late 1980s, the pavilion has remained an integral part of the Knowsley Road scene and the oldest surviving part of the ground, a monument to the foresight of club officials in the Roaring Twenties.

Monday, 7th May, 1962	Price 3d.

St. Helens	S.H.A.P.E. INDIANS
Full Back	**Full Back**
1 DONOVAN	1 OTIS FORSTER
Threequarters	**Threequarters**
2 VAN VOLLENHOVEN	2 GENE HILL
3 BRIERS	3 AL HAM
4 NORTHEY	4 TONY HOPPE
5 LARGE	5 FRANKLIN
Half Backs	**Half Backs**
6 BEDDOW	6 HAL RAY
7 FINNEY	7 JOHN DOP

Forwards	**Forwards**
8 LEYLAND	8 JIM BELLEMBAM
9 DAGNALL	9 DAVE BARRY
10 WATSON	10 RODNEY LE FAITZ
11 FRENCH	11 JOAN RHEINHART
12 CASE	12 CLEVE WRIGHT
13 MAJOR, W.	13 EDDY WEST

Referee : Mr. K. R. RATHBONE, St. Helens

Touch Judges: W. J. Greenhalgh (Red)   E. Lea (Orange)

S.H.A.P.E. Indians were one of the more unusual visitors to Knowsley Road. The team members worked in various types of administrative jobs in Paris at S.H.A.P.E. (Strategic Headquarters Army Personnel Europe), having played American football in high school or college. Coached by Russell Mericle, a former American footballer at West Point, the team had some experience of Rugby League, having beaten a French Army select XIII before embarking for England. The inexperienced Americans put up quite a good show, although they were overwhelmed by Tom Van Vollenhoven, who scored 7 tries and a goal in his team's 43-8 success.

A typical programme cover from the sixties. This particular issue commemorated the opening of the club's new floodlight system, officially switched on by Sir Harry (later Lord) Pilkington. The lighting scheme, similar to the installation at Leicester Rugby Union Club, consisted of powerful tungsten iodine lamps, arranged in five groups of ten on each side of the field. The system cost £10,923 and proved a real boon for the provision of midweek matches in winter. A new competition, the BBC Floodlit Trophy, became part of the fixture list, with the Saints contesting the inaugural final against Castleford at Knowsley Road on Tuesday 14 December 1965. The Yorkshiremen won 4-0 in front of over 11,000 fans.

Programme

Published by the ST. HELENS RUGBY F.C. LTD.

DIRECTORS

H. B. COOK, (Chairman)   F. C. DROMGOOLE (Vice-Chairman)
F. S. BROWN, S. HALL, H. J. HUNTER, C. MARTIN, A. NAYLOR,
J. ROBINSON, H. STOTT, L. SWIFT, F. YEARSLEY, J. YEARSLEY
J. SEDDON, Company Sec.   B. LOWE, Club Sec.

ST. HELENS
versus
Other Nationalities

Wednesday, 27th January, 1965
Kick-off 7-15 p.m.

Price   -   -   -   Threepence

Alexander the Great. The packed Main Stand forms an impressive backdrop as the world's finest scrum-half weaves his magic during the 25-10 victory over the 1961 New Zealand tourists at Knowsley Road. For the major part of his testimonial season in 1965/66, Murphy was switched to centre, yet still remained the complete footballer.

Three years before and the new Main Stand takes shape. Its overhanging design at the rear was necessary to overcome the problem of the adjacent railway cutting. This was a local line which took coal from Gillars Green Colliery to a nearby power station. The area is now filled in and serves as a car park. On Wednesday 1 March 1990 the shortest game at Knowsley Road took place. The league match against Warrington was abandoned after only four minutes on the grounds of health and safety when a section of sheeting broke away from the side of the Main Stand and embedded itself in the pitch, narrowly missing Warrington winger Des Drummond! Vouchers were issued for the replayed match a fortnight later, which was won 24-13 by Warrington in front of a crowd of 10,270.

International Rugby League at Knowsley Road as Great Britain defeat France 29-14 on 10 April 1957. A huge crowd of 23,250 look on as Warrington's stand-off Ray Price – later to become a Saint – scores another three-pointer. Barrow's ex-St Helens second rower Jack Grundy is the other British player in support. Knowsley Road was also a venue for the centenary World Cup in 1995, when New Zealand defeated Papua New Guinea by 22-6 in a Group Two match on Friday 13 October in front of nearly 9,000 fans.

If needs must. The scoreboard operator was forced to improvise during the Saints' club record 112-0 victory over Carlisle in a Lancashire Cup first round tie on Sunday 13 September 1986 – the biggest victory by a St Helens side. Centre Paul Loughlin kicked a club record 16 goals and finished with 40 points, another record.

Nine
The Great Entertainers
1978-1995

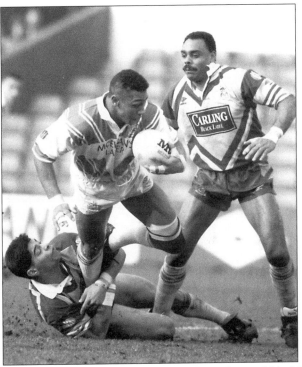

Welsh winger Anthony Sullivan in tearaway action in Saints' incredible 32-12 success against Leeds at Headingley in the second round of the Challenge Cup in 1991, a magnificent exhibition of attacking football. Unfortunately, defeat in the next round against their nemesis Wigan at Knowsley Road thwarted the prospect of Wembley glory for another year. Although gaining a reputation for fast, open and instinctive football, the St Helens club never really dominated the game like they always threatened to do, especially in the late 1980s and early 1990s, when Widnes and Wigan took the lion's share of major honours. The tag of perennial bridesmaids was a frustrating one to bear, yet at times the rugby was simply magical.

A moment to savour as St Helens defeat Wigan 10-4 in the Premiership final in 1993. Saints players gather round prop Kevin Ward, who suffered a horrendous ankle injury during the drawn league match at Central Park, Wigan, five weeks before. A tremendous competitor, Wardy's career ended as a result of the injury and it was to be many months – and many operations – before he was to regain anything like full fitness. Fate also dealt a cruel blow to drop-goal king Gus O'Donnell (second right), who was forced to give up the game he loved as a result of serious kidney problems.

The Saints celebrated the game's centenary in 1995 by reverting back to their original colours of blue and white striped jerseys. Although the winter centenary season itself was rather disappointing, with defeat against Wigan in the final of the Regal Trophy, the club was assembling a squad capable of being a major force in the future Super League. Scrum-half Bobbie Goulding (left) marshalled a rich crop of youngsters such as Steven Prescott, Joey Hayes, Danny Arnold and hooker Kieron Cunningham, mixed with experienced campaigners like Alan Hunte and Anthony Sullivan, together with ex-Rugby Union stars Scott Gibbs and Apollo Perelini. The world record fee of £250,000 for centre Paul Newlove in November 1995 was another indication that top honours would return to Knowsley Road once again.

Dressing room celebrations after the Saints' magnificent 26-18 Lancashire Cup final success over Wigan at Central Park on 28 October 1984, the club's first major trophy for seven years. Winger Sean Day, whose try and 5 goals helped his team to victory, is second from the left. A deadly marksman, Day led the goal-kicking (157) and points-scoring charts (362) in what was his first full season in the professional code in 1984/85. His super-cool penalty goal in the second half of the final did much to settle jangling nerves and bring the cup back to St Helens.

In the Lancashire Cup final of 1991 St Helens were victorious again, this time 24-14 over Rochdale Hornets. Phil Veivers, playing in the unaccustomed stand-off position, is about to touch down for one of his two tries. St Helens lifted the county cup for the eleventh, and last time, with a further brace of tries from George Mann, and a try and two goals from scrum-half Paul Bishop. The Saints' spectacular 28-16 victory over deadly rivals Wigan in the semi-final at Knowsley Road was watched by over 17,000 fans.

A team photograph in front of a packed Main Stand for the Challenge Cup third round tie on Sunday 11 March 1984. The rain lashes down as St Helens slump to a 7-16 defeat at the hands of Wigan. From left to right, back row: Clive Griffiths, Tony Burke, Andy Platt, Paul Round, Peter Gorley, Chris Arkwright, Roy Haggerty. Front row: Steve Rule, Steve Peters, Harry Pinner (captain), Graham Liptrot, Barrie Ledger, Neil Holding. The attendance at this game

was 20,007, the first time that this magical figure had been reached since September 1967, when former Saints' great Alex Murphy made his first appearance as a player at Knowsley Road after his transfer to Leigh. Ironically, Murphy was Wigan's coach in 1984 and engineered an unlikely success for his new charges in the final quarter of a rousing cup-tie, despite a magnificent Barrie Ledger try which seemed to have given the home side the edge.

Australian superstar Mal Meninga shows a clean pair of heels to Hull KR defenders Clark and Fairbairn on his way to a sensational eighty-yard interception try. Witness the excitement on the bench and television commentator Elton Welsby pointing the way to the line. This was Meninga's second interception in the match, from an over-ambitious lofted pass from Rovers' loose forward Hall, and a vital one too. Rovers were back in with a shout at 22-16 until the giant Aussie centre struck again. St Helens ran out winners 36-16.

Injury-hit St Helens slumped to a 38-14 defeat by Widnes in the 1988 Premiership final. Hard-running, second row forward Roy Haggerty scores a consolation try for St Helens, watched by referee John Holdsworth. This was their biggest ever defeat in a major final. Full-back Paul Loughlin kicked 3 goals in front of a crowd of over 35,000, with Saints' other touchdown registered by flying winger Barrie Ledger.

New Zealand stand-off Tea Ropati boots over one of his four goals for the Saints in their Lancashire Cup-tie at Barrow on Sunday 13 September 1992. Tea took over the kicking role in the absence of Paul Loughlin, who was sidelined with a broken arm. Tremendously strong and mobile, with superb handling skills, Ropati was the unanimous choice of his fellow Stones Bitter Championship players as the First Division Player of the Year for 1993, ahead of Wigan's Phil Clarke and Andy Platt. Tea was the Saints' only ever-present in the 1992/93 campaign, scoring 134 points, including 21 tries. Ropati left Knowsley Road at the end of the 1993/94 campaign to link-up with the fledgling Auckland Warriors in the city of his birth.

The Kiwi influence was extended at Knowsley Road in February 1990 with the appointment of Mike McClennan as coach. He is seen here directing operations on the training pitch. New Zealand centre Jarrod McCracken (17) listens intently in what was his first training session for the club. Mike took his 'McEwan's Lager Saints', as he liked to call them, to a Challenge Cup final in 1991, two Premiership finals and two Lancashire Cup finals. They also tied with Wigan at the top of the First Division table in 1992/93, only for the Riversiders to win on points difference. After leaving St Helens in 1994, Mike returned as coach of the Tonga side in the 1995 centenary World Cup.

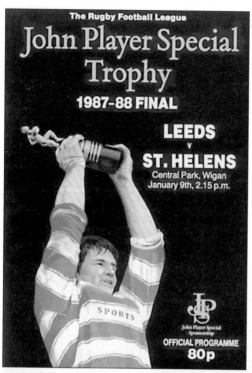

The programme for the 1988 John Player Trophy final, which was watched by over 16,000 spectators at Central Park, Wigan. This trophy had eluded St Helens since its inception in the 1971/72 season and Leeds, captained by Aussie prop Peter Tunks, were seen as formidable opponents. The Loiners led at half-time by 9-14, only for a dogged Saints fightback in the mud after the break. Centre Paul Loughlin's devastating two-try display, and two goals, earned him the coveted Man of the Match award and did much to secure his selection for the Australian tour at the end of the season. Scrum-half Neil Holding's drop-goal also proved to be the eventual difference between two evenly matched sides. The Saints' season ended on a disappointing note with a 38-14 loss to Widnes in the Premiership final at Old Trafford.

Neil 'Bomber' Holding had a superb match against Leeds in the 1988 John Player Trophy Final. He is seen here making one of several crucial breaks during the eighty minutes, despite the difficult conditions underfoot, leaving Leeds second rower Roy Powell in his wake. The ever-loyal Roy Haggerty and Phil Veivers are on hand to support. The John Player Trophy was the only major honour won by coach Alex Murphy on his return to Knowsley Road in the mid-1980s.

Loose forward Harry Pinner weaves his magic during the 1985 Premiership final against Hull KR at Elland Road. In the seventy-second minute he crowned a stunning Man of the Match performance by selling an outrageous dummy and waltzing past six bemused Hull KR defenders for the sixth St Helens try. Pinner's leadership qualities and handling skills had been so vital to the Saints' 36-16 success and he gleefully accepted the Premiership Trophy on behalf of his team-mates on his 300th appearance for the club. St Helens-born Pinner remains one of the game's greatest creative loose forwards. He made 322 appearances for the Saints, scoring 78 tries and 137 goals. A Great Britain tourist in 1984 (together with team-mate Neil Holding), he also captained his country in Test match Rugby League against France and New Zealand. After enjoying a successful testimonial at St Helens, he moved on to Widnes in the 1986/87 campaign in exchange for John Fieldhouse. He later joined Bradford Northern and coached at Wigan for a spell.

Good to be back. Alex Murphy poses for the cameras at Knowsley Road after his appointment as coach in November 1985. Murphy's teams played with great passion and threw the ball about in great style, reaching two Challenge Cup finals and finishing as runners-up in the First Division Championship in 1986/87 and 1987/88.

The Saints in 1986/87, when they were Challenge Cup finalists and First Division runners-up. From left to right, back row: Steve Halliwell, Paul Forber, Paul Round, Paul Loughlin, Chris Arkwright, Phil Veivers, Tony Burke, Alex Murphy (coach). Middle row: Eric Leach (kit), Shaun Allen, Kevin McCormack, Andy Platt, Graham Liptrot, Harry Pinner (captain), Roy Haggerty, Mark Bailey, Dave Chisnall (assistant coach). Front row: Paul Doherty, Barrie Ledger, Neil Holding, David Harrison.

A former ballboy at Knowsley Road, Gary Connolly played at Wembley as a seventeen-year-old amateur during the Saints' 27-0 defeat by Wigan in 1989, a tough call for one so young. However, the full-back showed his class with a sensational last-ditch tackle on Joe Lydon late on in the match which suggested great things were going to come his way. Sure enough, he developed into one of the best centres in the British game over the next few years, making his Great Britain debut as a substitute against Papua New Guinea in 1991. Supremely confident, with a resolute defence and excellent finishing skills, Connolly's try helped to beat Wigan in the 1993 Premiership final at Old Trafford. Unfortunately, his transfer to Wigan shortly afterwards severely dented Saints' team-building plans.

Centre Paul Loughlin takes the ball up against Doncaster at the start of the 1994/95 campaign. Loughlin progressed through the junior ranks and had established himself as a centre in the 1986/87 season, when he led the goal-kickers' chart with 190, no less than 63 ahead of his nearest rival, Paul Bishop, of Warrington. Loughlin was selected for the 1988 Great Britain tour to Australia and established a tremendous partnership at club level with ex-Barrow winger Les Quirk. A powerful runner, who could time a pass to perfection, he made 297 appearances for the Saints, kicking 842 goals, making him third in the all-time list behind Kel Coslett and George Lewis. He enjoyed a well-earned testimonial before joining Bradford Bulls, with Bernard Dwyer and Sonny Nickle as part of the world record deal which saw Paul Newlove come to Knowsley Road in 1995.

You beauty! Skipper and loose forward Shane Cooper raises the Premiership Trophy aloft after the 10-4 defeat of arch-rivals Wigan at a wet and windy Old Trafford on Sunday 16 May 1993. The £18,000 prize money is about to be handed over by Rugby League chief executive Maurice Lindsay. It was to be the last major honour won by the club before the arrival of Super League in 1996 and a fitting tribute to Shane Cooper, who had been the major on-field influence since his arrival five years before.

Ten
Sunshine Supermen
and Super League
1996-2000

It's a dog's life. One of the enduring images of summer rugby in the newly-formed Super League of 1996 was the club's new match day mascot, (Saint) Bernard.

St Helens trounce Warrington 66-14 on Sunday 26 August 1996. The last match of the season at Knowsley Road in front of over 18,000 fans saw the Saints clinch the inaugural Super League title. Aussie second rower Derek McVey scores one of his side's thirteen touchdowns, much to the delight of the Popular Side.

Something to celebrate. The Saints went through the 1996 season winning all their home matches in the European Super League, scoring 565 points and conceding a miserly 118 – the stuff champions are made of. The average crowd of 10,220 was an increase of 3,078 on the previous centenary season. The Saints scored over 50 points on no less than 7 occasions at Knowsley Road. Sheffield Eagles, Oldham, Castleford, Workington, Paris St Germain, Halifax and Warrington were the unfortunate victims of the St Helens attacking machine. Great Britain centre Paul Newlove led the try-scoring charts with 38, with Bobbie Goulding the League's number one marksman with 162 goals. This was only the second time – since Len Killeen in 1966 – that St Helens players have topped both charts. Goulding also raced to the fastest century of goals from the start of a season.

Paris St Germain are crushed 52-10 on Sunday 2 June 1996. St Helens second rower Apollo Perelini executes the perfect hand-off against the visitors' Pascal Jampy. Paris St Germain, who included a smattering of Australian players in their ranks, became the first French team to play in a competitive match at Knowsley Road since St Gaudens, in the ill-fated 'European Championship' clash in 1971. Signed from Western Samoan Rugby Union in May 1994 and nicknamed 'The Terminator', Perelini played a major role in the Saints' cup and league trophy double to earn the Rugby League Writers' Association Player of the Year award, which was richly deserved. A tough, durable front rower, Perelini made the crucial break which led to Kevin Iro's match-winning try in the 1999 Grand Final against the Bradford Bulls. A deeply religious person, Apollo always took to the field with a cross emblazoned on his left wristband.

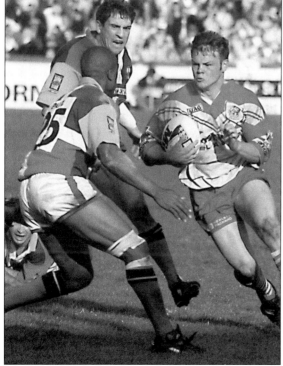

A typically powerful surge from local lad Kieron Cunningham leaves the Londoners' defence in tatters as the Broncos are beaten 24-22 on Sunday 12 May 1996. The elusive number nine was an inspirational figure during the club's Super League Championship campaign. A popular choice as Young Player of the Year, a place on the 1996 New Zealand tour with the Great Britain squad was a further reward for his efforts. The brother of former Saints' great of the seventies Eddie Cunningham, Kieron had developed into one of the world's great number nines by Super League IV. Good hands, solid in the tackle and with the pace and power to score tries from 50 metres if necessary, Kieron was seen as a vital part of maintaining the Saints' success in Super League well into the twenty-first century.

St Helens versus Warrington in 1996. Seemingly even larger than life on the big screen, skipper Bobbie Goulding addresses the crowd after receiving the Super League trophy to complete a memorable double of League and Challenge Cup, the first Saints' player to do so since Kel Coslett twenty years before. A charismatic figure and capable tactician, Goulding was instrumental in bringing his team back from the brink of defeat in the 1996 Challenge Cup final against Bradford Bulls, when his three towering bombs brought three tries in just seven minutes to totally change the course of the match. A renowned tactical kicker, his lateral runs brought players like Paul Newlove onto the ball with devastating effect, a particular feature of the first Super League season. Goulding's love affair with the Knowsley Road club lasted until the latter part of Super League III, when a series of disciplinary problems made a parting of the ways inevitable. Goulding looked to re-launch his career with the Huddersfield Giants, who appointed Mal Reilly as coach for the 1999 Super League season. The Yorkshire club already had its own former St Helens enclave, with forwards Jon Neill, Ian Pickavance, full-back Danny Arnold and Great Britain centre Paul Loughlin on the books, with Phil Veivers as assistant coach.

'Battle royal' would not be wide of the mark to describe these scenes in the St Helens versus Wigan fourth round Challenge Cup clash at Knowsley Road in 1997. The Saints won 26-12, despite being reduced to twelve men, following the dismissal of scrum-half Bobbie Goulding for a high tackle. The resulting brawl resulted in both clubs being fined a record £15,000, of which half was suspended for twelve months.

One of the young guns hoping to carry on the Saints' tradition of great three-quarters into the next century. Wigan-born Anthony Stewart progressed through the Academy and Alliance teams at Knowsley Road, making his first team debut against Salford in the first round of the Premiership Trophy in 1997. He earned a place in the final itself against Wigan at Old Trafford and came even more into the spotlight when he gave Australian superstar Wendell Sailor the runaround in the World Club Championship quarter-final against Brisbane Broncos, down under. An academy international, Anthony became a valuable squad member in the fourth Super League campaign. Equally adept at centre or wing, his pace and increasing strength augured much promise for the future.

The mighty Paul Newlove fires out a pass to his winger in the St Helens versus Warrington Wolves match on 23 May 1999. The inevitable result was a try for winger Anthony Sullivan, one of ten in the Saints' 57-20 success. The signing of Paul Newlove was one of the most important in the club's history. His transfer from Bradford Bulls in November 1995 was reckoned to be worth £500,000. The Great Britain centre moved in exchange for the former Saints' trio of Paul Loughlin, Sonny Nickle and Bernard Dwyer, as well as £250,000, a record cash-plus-players deal. His signing was the trigger the club needed for success in the newly-formed Super League competition in the summer of 1996. Newlove finished the campaign as the leading try-scorer with 38 touchdowns, 9 more than his nearest rivals, Gary Atkins of Hull KR and Wigan's Jason Robinson. Newlove helped his team-mates to back-to-back Challenge Cup final successes against the Bradford Bulls in 1996 and 1997 as the Saints established themselves as a major force in the modern game. Great strength and incredibly balanced running at pace are two of Newlove's qualities. He is also a great wingman's centre and his combination with Anthony Sullivan is arguably the most potent club pairing of the late 1990s. Indeed, their attacking potential was seen at its most effective during the 37-22 defeat of London Broncos at the Stoop on Friday 18 September 1998, when Anthony Sullivan scorched in for five touchdowns courtesy of his centre partner, equalling the Super League match record. Newlove took over as Super League's top scorer with 52 in 59 matches after Super League III, a tremendous testimony to his attacking ability. However, it is his pace which is so impressive for a big man and the 1999 campaign saw several instances of near length-of-the-field finishes for touchdowns, some from interceptions. Truly one of the Knowsley Road club's all-time greats, Newlove remained a quiet, unassuming figure, capable of providing that little bit extra when the chips were down.

New faces at Knowsley Road for Super League IV: Ellery Hanley (left) was a sensational choice as coach to replace Australian Shaun McRae. He was able to add the power and workrate of international second rower Sonny Nickle to his squad. A former Saint, who left for Bradford Bulls as part of the Paul Newlove deal in 1995, Sonny proved to be a fine acquisition second time around.

Paul Sculthorpe joined the St Helens club in December 1997 in a £375,000 deal from Warrington Wolves, a world record for a forward, with former Saint Chris Morley moving to Wilderspool as part of the deal. Although essentially a loose forward, Scully could occupy any position in the back row with distinction. Paul was already a seasoned Great Britain international when he moved to Knowsley Road and was a member of the 1996 party which toured Papua New Guinea, Fiji and New Zealand in 1996. Good hands, capable of prodigious tackling stints and the ability to read a game made him a big favourite at St Helens. Very much an old head on young shoulders, he was seen as a future captain and one of the cornerstones of the club's challenge for honours into the new millennium. Paul was also very much the ideal role model for any aspiring professional players.

A stunning finale to the 1999 Super League season and the century as the Bradford Bulls are defeated 8-6 in front of 50,717 fans at Old Trafford, Manchester, on Saturday 9 October. Skipper Chris Joynt holds the trophy aloft, to the delight of the travelling army of St Helens supporters. Bradford had begun as favourites and scored the first try at the end of the first quarter. However, coach Ellery Hanley's boys produced some magnificent scrambling defence to keep the Bulls at bay, with a Sean Long penalty reducing the deficit to four points just before half-time. After a superb run from prop Apollo Perelini in the sixty-fifth minute, the ball was swept out wide for centre Kevin Iro to score in the corner. Sean Long's magnificent touchline conversion sailed straight between the uprights, as good a kick as any in Saints' history. There may well have been a smash and grab element in their success, yet rarely has a St Helens team shown such steel in defence. An unforgettable occasion.